The How-To Book of the

MASS

The How-To Book of the

MASS

*Everything You Need to Know
But No One Ever Taught You*

Michael Dubruiel

Our Sunday Visitor Publishing Division
Our Sunday Visitor, Inc.
Huntington, Indiana 46750

Nihil Obstat
Rev. Michael Heintz
Censor Librorum

Imprimatur
✠ John M. D'Arcy
Bishop of Fort Wayne-South Bend
October 31, 2006

Our Sunday Visitor Publishing Division
Our Sunday Visitor, Inc.
200 Noll Plaza
Huntington, IN 46750

ISBN: 978-1-59276-269-9 (Inventory No. T322)
LCCN: 2002107484

Cover design by Tyler Ottinger
Interior design by Sherri L. Hoffman
Art by Kevin Davidson

PRINTED IN THE UNITED STATES OF AMERICA

Dedication

This book is dedicated to all priests who, throughout their ministry in the Church, have celebrated the Mass with great reverence and dignity. Through their unselfish service to God, they have helped untold multitudes to come closer to Christ and His Church. May the Lord richly bless them in His kingdom!

I especially want to mention those priests whose
piety has touched me personally and moved me away
from sin and toward our Lord:

Bishop Robert Baker
Archabbot Lambert Reilly, O.S.B.
Father Stanley Skora +
Father Jerome Palmer, O.S.B. +
Father Joseph Doyle, S.J.
Father John Finnegan +
Father Benedict J. Groeschel, C.F.R.
and
Venerable Father Solanus Casey, O.F.M. Cap. +
(who saved my life)

I also wish to dedicate this book to:

My great-grandfather Frank Smoski + who always had tears
in his eyes when he came back from Holy Communion, teaching me
a valuable lesson as a child that I have never forgotten.

My grandfather Alexander Dubruiel + who prayed the Rosary
in the last years of his life openly and unashamedly, giving me
a great example of manhood.

My grandfather Bernard Polaski + who taught me as we fished
on the banks of the Ashuelot River in southern New Hampshire that what
happens at Mass is something that extends to every second of our lives.

Please pray for all of them and, in the case of
Venerable Solanus Casey, to him, as you read this book!

(+ *deceased*)

Contents

Preface   15

Introduction   19
Understanding the Mass
Helpful Hints and Information
Differences
Encountering Jesus Christ at Mass

What *Is* the Mass?   25
Where Does the Term "Mass" Come From?
What Is Liturgy?
Other Names for the Mass
So, What *Is* the Mass?

How to Get Something Out of Mass   29
What Type of *Son* Block Are You Wearing?
SP 1: Your Head Is Blocked
SP 2: Your Chest Is Blocked
SP 3: Your Whole Body Is Blocked

1. How to Enter the Church   37
The Origin of the Mass
Our Response
Opening the Door
Holy Water
Blessing Yourself
Genuflecting vs. Bowing
Kneeling or Sitting
Becoming Aware of God's Presence
Meditation — "… Jesus himself drew near and went with them."

2. How to Celebrate the Opening Rites   49
The Opening Hymn

The Procession
The Sign of the Cross and the Greeting
Meditation — " 'What is this conversation ...?' "

3. How to Celebrate the Penitential Rite   59
Preparation
Silence
The *Confiteor*
Striking Our Breast
Pray for Me
Other Options
May Almighty God Forgive You!
Lord, Have Mercy (*Kyrie*)
Meditation — "… we had hoped …"

4. How to Sing the Gloria   69
Gloria in Excelsis
When the Gloria Is Omitted
The Song of the Angels
What Is the "Glory" of God?
Putting God First
Meditation — "… a vision of angels …"

5. How to Say "Amen" to the Opening Prayer   79
Let Us Pray
Silence
The Collect
Saying "Amen"

6. How to Understand the Liturgy of the Word   85
The Two Parts of the Mass
The Covenant at Mount Sinai
The New Covenant of Jesus
The Liturgy of the Word
Meditation — "… and slow of heart to believe …"

7. How to Listen to the First Reading   93
Where Is This Reading Taken From?
The Old Testament
A Secret About the First Reading

Easter Time — A Reading From Acts
Our Response

8. How to Respond to the Responsorial Psalm   101
What Are Psalms?
Reference to Christ?
The Prayer of Jesus
The Psalm Response
Our Response

9. How to Listen to the Second Reading   109
Where Is the Second Reading Taken From?
Continuous Reading
Letters Written to Churches and the Church
Our Response

10. How to Listen to the Gospel   115
The Gospel Acclamation — Alleluia
When the Alleluia Is Replaced
The Good News
Preparation of the Deacon or Priest to Proclaim the Gospel
Guarding Our Minds, Lips, and Hearts
The Proclamation of the Gospel
Our Response

11. How to Hear a Great Homily *Every Time* You Attend Mass   125
What Is a Homily?
Praying for the Preacher
Listening to a Homily
Meditation — "… [Jesus] interpreted to them in all the
    scriptures …"

12. Time Out! Where Are *They* Going and Who Are They?   133
Dismissal of Catechumens
Responding to the Word
Praying for the Catechumens and Candidates
Where Are They Going?
Meditation — " 'Stay with us …' "

13. How to Pray the Creed 139

The Response of the Faithful
I Believe ...
... In One God
... In Jesus Christ
... In the Holy Spirit and the Catholic Church
... In the Resurrection of the Body and Life Everlasting
Renewal of Baptismal Promises
Meditation — "He appeared to be going further ..."

14. How to Pray the Prayers of the Faithful 149

Acting on Faith
Lord, Hear Our Prayer
Universal Prayer
Meditation — "... they constrained him ..."

15. How to Join in the Preparation of the Gifts 155

The Liturgy of the Eucharist
The Collection
Preparation of the Altar
Procession of the Gifts Hymn
Procession of the Gifts
Blessing the Bread and the Wine
Hand Washing
Our Offering
Our Response
Prayer Over the Gifts
Meditation — "... he took the bread and blessed ..."

16. How to Give Thanks to God in the Eucharistic Prayer 167

The Eucharistic Prayers
The Preface
The *Sanctus*
Kneeling
Epiclesis
The Institutional Narrative and Consecration
The *Anamnesis* (Memorial)
The Mystery of Faith
Intercessions

17. How to Say "Amen" to the Eucharistic Prayer   179

    The Doxology
    The Great Amen
    The Assent of the Faithful
    Making the Amen Our Own

18. How to Pray the Lord's Prayer   183

    Praying as Jesus Taught
    "Our Father, who art in heaven"
    "Hallowed be thy name"
    "Thy kingdom come"
    "Thy will be done on earth as it is in heaven"
    "Give us this day our daily bread"
    "Forgive us our trespasses as we forgive"
    "And lead us not into temptation"
    "But deliver us from evil"
    Deliver Us, Lord
    For the Kingdom

19. How to Give the Sign of Peace   193

    Grant Us the Peace and Unity of Your Kingdom
    My Peace I Give You!
    Sharing Peace

20. How to Witness the Breaking of the Bread   197

    The Breaking of the Bread
    Lamb of God ...
    Beating Your Breast?
    By This Mingling ...
    Meditation — "... and broke it ..."

21. How to Receive Holy Communion   203

    Behold the Lamb of God ...
    Our Response
    Preparation to Receive the Eucharist
    Processing to the Altar
    Receiving the Eucharist
    Contemplating the Fruits of Holy Communion
    Prayer After Communion
    Meditation — "And their eyes were opened ..."

22. How to Receive the Final Blessing   213
Concluding Rites
Final Blessing
Sent Forth in Peace

23. How to Leave the Church and Evangelize   217
The Closing Procession
Exiting From Your Seat or Pew
Encountering the Usher and Celebrant
The World
Meditation — "And they rose that same hour ..."

Appendix I: Prayers Before Mass   223
Prayer of Saint Ambrose
Prayer of Saint Thomas Aquinas
Prayer to the Blessed Virgin Mary
Prayer to Saint Joseph
Prayer to All Angels and Saints

Appendix II: Prayers After Mass   227
Prayers of Saint Ignatius of Loyola
    Anima Christi
    Prayer of Self-Dedication to Jesus Christ (*Suscipe*)
Prayer Before a Crucifix
Prayer of Saint Thomas Aquinas
Prayer of Saint Bonaventure
Universal Prayer of Pope Clement XI
Prayer to the Blessed Virgin Mary
Prayer to Saint Joseph
Prayer in Honor of the Day's Saint

Appendix III: Study Guide   235

Appendix IV: Where Can I Learn More?   261
Books
Video/CD-ROM
Internet

About the Author   267

"Blessed is he who shall eat bread in the kingdom of God!"
— Luke 14:15

Each time the Mass is offered, the fruits of our Redemption are poured anew upon our souls. By uniting ourselves with the sacred rite of the Mass, and above all by receiving Holy Communion, we enter into the sacrifice of Christ. We mystically die with the divine Victim and rise again with Him to new life in God. We are freed from our sins, we are once again pleasing to God, and we receive grace to follow Him more generously in the life of charity and fraternal union which is the life of His Mystical Body.

— Thomas Merton, *The Living Bread*

When the Church celebrates the Eucharist, the memorial of her Lord's death and resurrection, this central event of salvation becomes really present and "the work of our redemption is carried out." This sacrifice is so decisive for the salvation of the human race that Jesus Christ offered it and returned to the Father only *after he had left us a means of sharing in it* as if we had been present there. Each member of the faithful can thus take part in it and inexhaustibly gain its fruits.

— Pope John Paul II, *Ecclesia de Eucharistia*

The Eucharist, as the presence of the cross, is the abiding tree of life, which is ever in our midst and ever invites us to take the fruit of true life.

— Pope Benedict XVI, *"In the Beginning ..."*

Preface

Since the original publication of this book in 2002, I made my first-ever pilgrimage to Rome and to the Basilica of Saint Peter in February of 2006. Traveling with me were my wife, Amy, and our children. The youngest, Michael Jacob, 15 months old at the time, spent most of that week traveling on my back in a child carrier.

As soon as we arrived in Rome and dropped our baggage off at the apartment that would be our home for the next nine days, we hurried off to the Vatican and Saint Peter's only three blocks away. For a few minutes, we just stood there. How much of what we had studied, wrote about, and experienced in our lives originated within this holy spot!

Like the ancient pilgrims setting out for Jerusalem, the words of the Psalmist came to mind:

I rejoiced with those who said to me,
"Let us go to the house of the Lord!"
And now we have set foot
within your gates ....
— Psalm 122:1-2, *Christian Community Bible*

Indeed, the colonnades of Bernini seemed to embrace us and invite us into the basilica. But there was a problem, as we were all very tired and the security line stretched around those same colonnades. After some discussion, and watching the speed at which the line moved, we decided that we hadn't traveled all this way to sleep — a theme that would recur throughout our novena of days in Rome (and no doubt responsible for the bout of walking pneumonia that I later spent the remainder of Lent 2006 recovering from).

The line moved quickly, and in no time we were in another line that, "like sheep," we stood and waited in; it was a line that took us into the crypt of Saint Peter's, past the tombs of the popes — that of the most recently deceased pope, John Paul II, to the first pope, Saint Peter. We stopped at Pope John Paul II's tomb (along with the crowd of pilgrims) and asked his intercession for a variety of needs. Then we passed by the *confessio* of Saint Peter and likewise prayed, and I reflected on the many scenes of the Gospel that speak of the humanness of Peter and his desire to follow Christ.

Next we found ourselves outside of the crypt of the basilica and unsure of where we were. We blindly followed a few other pilgrims back up the stairs of Saint Peter's, and this time found the way into the massive church.

Entering the basilica, we walked through the large doors and were suddenly within a sacred space whose image I have seen in pictures and on television thousands of times. Amazing! Thoughts of the Second Vatican Council that took place here, which gave us the reform of the liturgy and especially the Mass, flooded my mind.

On this first visit, we slowly walked through, taking it all in. We knew that Jeffrey Kirby, a seminarian from South Carolina who was studying at the North American College in Rome, would be giving us a guided tour the next day. So this was just a "walk through," a sort of get-acquainted visit.

I had Michael Jacob in the baby carrier on my back, and when we had walked about halfway up the nave of the basilica, I darted into a side chapel where the Blessed Sacrament was exposed for adoration and prayer. There were quite a few people in the chapel, a group representative of the Church: priests, brothers, nuns, lay people from a variety of places, but only one child — the one on my back.

I knelt in the back and thanked God for safely bringing us to our destination, and I asked for His blessing upon our time of prayer in the Eternal City. It was then that Michael Jacob spoke, uttering one word in his baby voice but very clearly: "Christ."

He said nothing else. He had never spoken that word before. At the time his vocabulary was pretty much limited to six or seven words, the most used of which was "No," which he spoke with great emphasis.

I arose, genuflected, and made my way back out into the nave of the basilica.

And I wondered.

Mass was going on in Spanish at the Chair of Saint Peter, and the Spanish cardinal who was presiding was preaching his homily. I gleaned that it was about Saint Peter, for the cardinal kept repeating in Spanish the profession of Saint Peter that led to Jesus declaring him the "rock" upon which He would build His Church, which in English is:

> *"You are the Christ, the Son of the living God."*
> — Matthew 16:16

Looking above the high altar of Saint Peter's, I saw our Lord's response to Peter's profession written in Latin in huge letters: "You are Peter, and on this rock I will build my church" (Matthew 16:18).

Then my little son's message hit me. This same Christ (Messiah, God's anointed, the Savior) that Saint Peter was able to recognize in Jesus is still with us in the Eucharist that comes to us through the ministry of the Church that our Lord founded upon Saint Peter. I knew and believed that before this moment, but hearing my young son declare it in Saint Peter's, in the presence of the Blessed Sacrament, was a real blessing to me and a great reminder of the origins of everything that this book is about.

This is a book about the Mass, the Christian Eucharist. Everything this book is about centers on Jesus Christ.

It was Jesus who chose the twelve apostles and made Peter their leader. It was Jesus who established His Church — who also said that it would be home to both "weeds and wheat," meaning "sinners and saints." It was Jesus who referred to this Church as His Bride — meaning all of us who are members are His alone. It was Jesus who gave us the Eucharist as His abiding presence to be received and adored.

It is my hope that as you both learn about the Mass and then experience this great mystery that our Lord left to His apostles, you may always hear "Christ" and remember that it is all about Him.

> *"For flesh and blood has not revealed this to you, but my Father who is in heaven."*
>
> — Matthew 16:17

Michael Dubruiel
Dedication of the Basilicas of
Saint Peter and Saint Paul, Apostles
November 18, 2006

Introduction

UNDERSTANDING THE MASS

You may be a lifelong Catholic or someone contemplating joining the Catholic Church. In either case, you will find in this book a simple guide to accompany you through every celebration of the Mass. Since it first appeared in 2002 as part of Our Sunday Visitor's "How-To" series, this book has helped many readers to come to a deeper understanding of what Catholics do every time they gather to celebrate the Lord's Eucharist.

This current edition of the book has been revised to build upon the original. A study guide has been added as an appendix so that groups using this book may now have review and reflection questions to use when they gather to discuss the contents. Other material has been added to reflect the release of a papal encyclical on the Eucharist, as well as the release of new books, such as my own *How to Get the Most Out of the Eucharist*, which have been released since the original publication of this book.

What remains constant is the careful detail given to each moment of the Mass, from the time you arrive at the door of the church until the time you exit the same door. You will find helpful advice to guide you in performing the various rituals associated with the Mass, as well as the reasons for performing these rituals. You also will find interesting facts about where various prayers and Readings of the Mass come from.

HELPFUL HINTS AND INFORMATION

The layout of this book is necessarily light. But at the same time it is packed with tons of useful aids, helping every experience of the Mass to be all that it is intended to be by our Lord and His Church.

To that end, there is boxed material throughout the book to help you understand:

Ancient words, items, and phrases used in the Mass.

Some of the words used in the Mass go back to the time of Jesus. They may seem obscure to us in the twenty-first century, but they are an unbroken thread that takes us all the way back to our Lord. There are also sacred items used in the ritual that may seem strange to you. Look for definitions identified as **What Does It Mean?** or **What Is It?** And **Who Is ...?** will explain the roles of those important to the early Church.

That the prayers that make up the Mass are from the Holy Bible.

Where Is It In Scripture? will help you make the connections between the various prayers and where they can be found in the Bible. Sometimes knowing these connections can help you to understand the prayers better.

That the parts of the Mass are ancient and go back to the practice of the early Church.

Material under **The Faith of the Early Church** illuminates a particular part of the Mass and how it was celebrated in the early Church.

Catholic beliefs.

"The way we pray is the way we believe," *Lex orandi, lex credendi*, is an ancient dictum. Throughout this book you will find references to the *Catechism of the Catholic Church* or the *Compendium of the Catechism of the Catholic*

olic Church that highlight beliefs of the Catholic Church as they relate to or are expressed in various parts of the Mass. These references are either marked *CCC* or *Compendium* and may be found in boxes entitled **Catechism of the Catholic Church.** Other aspects of the Catholic faith, such as prayers and parts of the Mass, are included under the heading **Catholic Beliefs** or **Catholic Practices.**

The variety of postures that Catholics take during the celebration of the Mass.

Boxes will explain **How To** … for certain postures, and in some cases what to say when you do them.

Ways to turn what might be negative feelings into positive!

Every Mass offers us special opportunities for grace. Each is identified as an **Opportunity for Spiritual Growth.** These are key moments in the Mass when we can consciously decide to "die to ourselves." They are meant to give us pause, to suspend judgment, and to be truly open to the Holy Spirit's action during every Mass.

DIFFERENCES

I travel throughout the United States quite a bit and attend Mass wherever I go, so I know that although one will always find the celebration of the Mass to be essentially the same, one will inevitably encounter differences. Some of these differences are allowed by the Church; some, quite honestly, are just well-meaning but unfortunate attempts to make the Mass more relevant to the local congregation.

I have stood for the national anthem in a Catholic church in Tennessee right after the entrance procession (which made me feel like I was at a sporting event). Closer to home, I attended a Mass during which a visiting priest never used one word from the official texts of the Mass, from the sign of the cross to the dismissal. (No small feat, I might add!). These experiences have unsettled me, as I would guess they would anyone else who has experienced the jarring effect of those who break with the familiarity of the ritual. There is something in the "sameness" of the Mass that is the very genius of the effectiveness of ritual. Hopefully, liturgists (those who make a living by coordinating the celebration of the Church's rituals) and presiders will soon figure this out.

But if you encounter such differences, I encourage you to make it an opportunity to "die" to yourself and let God be God. This is difficult, but it is an excellent way to turn a negative experience into a positive, spiritual one. If the abuse of the Mass ritual is serious, contact the pastor. If it continues, report it to the diocesan office of worship and the bishop, but make sure it really is abuse before taking that step.

Mindful of such differences, I have tried to include in this guide some variations that are allowed, though they might strike you as odd if you have gone to the same parish for most of your life.

ENCOUNTERING JESUS CHRIST AT MASS

There is more contained within these pages than just the mechanics of the celebration of the Mass; also described is how to attend Mass in a way that makes it truly an encounter with the Lord Jesus Christ every time. Lifelong Catholics may have grown so used to the ritual that they aimlessly go through the motions and find that their minds often wander. Novices, on the other hand, may feel so overwhelmed by all that is unknown to them that they fail to recognize Christ in the process.

Every encounter with Jesus is unique. When the apostles spied Jesus walking on the water, they were overcome with fear. Peter asked our Lord if it were really Him or a ghost.

Our Lord told the apostles not to fear. Peter, now having regained his composure, asked if he might join Jesus for His evening walk on the water.

Jesus told him to come out of the boat. And Peter did.

And Peter walked on the water, too.

For a few moments.

Then he took account of how strong the winds were, and he sank like a rock.

This morning when I went to Mass it was thundering outside. I wondered whether I had remembered to shut the windows at home and in my car. I thought about all the electrical appliances, the trees in our yard, and I wondered whether lightning had struck anywhere near our home. All the while, the priest was preaching his homily. Do you think I encountered the living Jesus at that moment?

Other times it is my one-year-old son, Michael Jacob, or five-year-old son, Joseph, who are vying for my attention. They can make listening and praying difficult. But on the other hand, they often help me to notice everything in a new light. Their pointing out everything they see and asking "What is it?" has been a great aid in the formation of this book.

Whatever the distractions of the day, I know that too often I am caught up with the winds and not with Jesus. If you are like me, then this book will help you.

The Mass is our opportunity to meet Jesus, to listen to Him and to receive Him. There is a story in the Gospel of Luke that provides a summary of the Mass. It is the account of how the Risen Lord Jesus made Himself known to several of His disciples as they were making their way to a town called Emmaus. As we look at the various parts of the Mass, we will pause to meditate on this story from Luke's Gospel. I expect that you will come to find in this Gospel story an excellent tool to help you refocus yourself on Christ at the various moments of every Mass you attend.

I have written this book with all Catholics in mind. Whether young or old, male or female, liberal or conservative — in Christ we are one, at Mass we are one, one Body: Jesus'. I hope to help you rediscover the Mass as a vehicle for letting go of all that can seem to separate you in life, and to replace what seem like distractions with the deep, meaning-filled events of your daily life. Rediscover the Mass as a way to open the wounds, the scars, the needs that Jesus can heal, and to encounter the very Lord Himself, so you might leave every Mass with His peace and a deep sense of unity with God and your fellow man.

What *Is* the Mass?

WHERE DOES THE TERM "MASS" COME FROM?

It is very possible that you may not know what "Mass" means. After all, you probably have always heard the Mass said in your own language. But "Mass" is derived from the way the Mass was ended in Latin.

WHAT DOES IT MEAN?

 "Mass" is an English rendering of the Latin term "missa." In Latin the Mass ends with "*Ite missa est,*" which translated into English means "Go, it is sent" — the "it" being the Church.

From the Latin word "*missa*" comes the English word "dismiss." So "Mass" means "dismissal." The celebration takes its name from the sending forth that occurs at the end of every Mass.

Because of the familiarity of the ending, the celebration of our Lord's Supper eventually became known simply as the "Mass." There were actually two dismissals in the celebration — one in which catechumens (people who were not fully Catholic yet but wanted to be) were dismissed right after the sermon (see "What Is It?" Page 40), and the dismissal at the end, when all the fully initiated Catholics, the faithful, were dismissed. There were two "Masses" — namely, the Mass of the Catechumens and the Mass of the Faithful.

The fact that we call this greatest of Christian prayers the "dismissal" points to the essence of what it means to be a follower of Jesus Christ. Our Lord calls us to Himself, and through His saving act invites us to a unity with God the Father through the power of His Holy Spirit. Jesus makes communion with God possible. But following Jesus does not stop with this communion, for once He has united us to Himself, He then sends us forth with a mission (a dismissal).

"Go" is one of His final words to His disciples as He ascends into heaven in the Gospel of Matthew's account (Matthew 28:19). Hence, the way every Mass ends with "go" is at the heart of what we come to the Mass for — to be empowered by God and sent forth again.

Saint Peter spoke up for the apostles in John's Gospel when Jesus asked the disciples whether they wanted to leave Him, too (like the others who couldn't bear it when He said He would give them His Flesh to eat — John 6). He said, "Lord, to whom shall we go? You have the words of eternal life; and we have believed, and have come to know, that you are the Holy One of God" (John 6:68-69).

The "go" that is the very meaning of the word "Mass" receives its meaning from our communion with our Lord Jesus Christ during the Mass, where we believe and come to know Him!

WHAT IS LITURGY?

It is common today to hear the Mass referred to as the liturgy.

Liturgy can refer to any public act that the Church celebrates. One of the ancient names for the Mass is the Divine Liturgy — literally, God's public service.

What in the past would have been referred to as the Mass of the Catechumens is now called the Liturgy of the Word, and what would have been called the Mass of the Faithful is now referred to as the Liturgy of the Eucharist. Eucharist is also a Greek word that means "thanksgiving." One of the central prayers in the second part of the Mass is a prayer of thanksgiving, and, of course, the Eucharist is also another name for the Blessed Sacrament.

OTHER NAMES FOR THE MASS

The original names for the Mass that were used in the early Church and later include:

• **The Breaking of the Bread,** referring to what Jesus did, not only at the Last Supper, but also when He revealed Himself to the disciples on the road to Emmaus and when He multiplied the loaves and the fishes to feed the multitudes.

- **The Lord's Supper,** referring to the meal that He shared with His apostles on the night before He died, when the Mass was instituted.
- **The Eucharist,** referring to another central act that Jesus did before He broke the bread — He gave thanks. Again "Eucharist" means "thanksgiving."
- **The Offering,** referring to what Jesus did upon the cross when He offered Himself to the Father for our salvation, and what He did at the Last Supper when He offered His Body and Blood to His apostles under the species of bread and wine.
- **The Holy Sacrifice,** referring to the sacrifice of our Lord at Cavalry, which the Mass makes present.

Each of these names carries with it some sense of what the celebration of the Mass is: a holy recalling of the sacrifice of Jesus that He offered God the Father during His last meal with His apostles on the night before He died. During that meal He took bread, gave thanks, broke the bread, and gave it to His disciples.

SO, WHAT IS THE MASS?

The *Catechism of the Catholic Church* defines the Mass by saying, "The Eucharist is the heart and the summit of the Church's life, for in it Christ associates his Church and all her members with his sacrifice of praise and thanksgiving offered once for all on the cross to his Father; by this sacrifice he pours out the graces of salvation on his Body which is the Church" (No. 1407).

The Church is the Body of Christ, and through the celebration of the Eucharist the Church becomes most fully what she is. We are present at the one sacrifice that Christ offered the Father, and we join our own sacrifices to His at every Mass.

The Mass is also a banquet. Offering our sacrifices to those of the Lord, we in return receive His Body and Blood and become more fully part of His Body here on earth.

Sometimes one aspect of the Mass is emphasized over another, but both are necessarily a part of the Mass. There can never be a meal where something has not been sacrificed and in turn becomes our food. The "Lamb that was slain" (Revelation 13:8) is the sacrifice that is offered at Mass and the meal that is served.

There is no act that we as Christians participate in during our earthly lives that is more important than this act!

How to Get Something Out of Mass

WHAT TYPE OF *SON* BLOCK ARE YOU WEARING?

It wasn't uncommon when I was growing up to hear one of my teenage friends tell his parents that he didn't want to go to Mass because he didn't "get anything out of it" and it bored him. "You're going anyway!" was usually the sharp rebuttal to such a complaint, which often gave me the impression that the parents didn't get anything out of it, either.

The complaint is heard often enough today that answering it merits a special place right at the beginning of this book. I do not agree with the maxim often leveled at people who complain — "perhaps you're not putting anything into the Mass" — primarily because it is false. The people usually voicing the complaint, young or old, have in fact put themselves there, but honestly have not gotten anything out of the Mass.

What, then, is my response?

If you are not getting anything out of the Mass, it is because *you have not opened yourself up to the great gift that God wishes to give you.* In other words, something is blocking your mind, your heart, or your soul. You obviously have applied too much *Son* block to either your head (covering your mind), your chest (covering your heart), or to your whole body (covering your soul).

When I lived in Florida, I was able to spend the entire day out in the scorching sun without getting burned. How? By applying a generous portion of sunblock (with a high SPF number) before going out, of course. "Son" block works the same, but in reverse. If we have too much "Son" block on our heads, chests, or bodies, we risk being burned worse than anything the sun could ever do to us. And the burning here is meant both figuratively and literally, both in this life and in the next.

It seems that in the time of Christ there were more than a few who were wearing a heavy layer of this Son block, and it prevented them from receiving His light. We can make the same mistake as those who walked on the same streets, in the same villages as our Lord during His earthly life. We block ourselves to His Presence and leave our encounter with Him at Mass untouched and unchanged. (At least to our own perception — we can never encounter our Lord and not really be untouched and unchanged!)

If you truly want to get something out of the Mass, you must remove whatever *Son* block you are wearing, and in the process you'll open your mind, heart, and soul to receive the rays of the Lord's grace. Here are some concrete ways to determine what part of you might be Son blocked and what you can do to remove it. There are three that I have termed SP 1, SP 2, and SP 3. The SP stands for "Son Prevention."

SP 1: YOUR HEAD IS BLOCKED

Some of us play an intellectual game at Mass of finding fault with the way the Mass is celebrated. We can be motivated to do this out of a false sense of piety born from a desire for "orthodoxy." But the Mass is not a place for us to sit back like movie critics and to find fault; rather, it is a place to encounter Jesus Christ.

Some of those who encountered the Son of God during His earthly ministry complained about His lowly estate. "Is not this the carpenter's son?" (Matthew 13:55) or "Can anything good come out of Nazareth?" (John 1:46).

When our Lord took on our human nature, as Saint Paul says, He "emptied himself, taking the form of a servant" (Philippians 2:7). Part of this lowering was being raised in Galilee. Galileans were considered unlettered and uneducated by the religious elite in Jerusalem. Recent Bible studies have revealed hints that Jesus was thought of in this way by some of His contemporaries. We also see this in the Scriptures themselves, when our Lord's Aramaic is not as perfect as the Jews living in Jerusalem would have spoken it. Examples of this are cited in the Lord's use of *"talitha kum"* for "little girl, get up"; the words He uses mistakenly mix the masculine with the feminine grammatically. It is also hinted at during His crucifixion when He cries out *"Eli, Eli, la'ma sabach-tha'ni?"* We are told it means, "My God, my God, why hast thou forsaken me?" (Matthew 27:46). But those residents of Jerusalem who heard Him say it did not understand, and thought He was invoking Elijah.

This might scandalize some of us who expect that if God were to become human, He would be perfect in every way. But a reading of the Gospels shows us that God truly lowered Himself, from being born in a cave to having "nowhere to lay his head" during His life on earth.

OPPORTUNITY FOR SPIRITUAL GROWTH

When you find yourself ready to judge another person or the way something is being done at Mass, turn the judgment into a prayer for the person or people who, a few seconds before, had been your victims. Ask God to bless them and to bless you through their service.

If we are waiting for the "perfect" priest to say the Mass for us, we will miss out on the great graces our Lord wishes to bring to us. The people who experienced Jesus walking on the face of the earth had their excuses. Surely this man was of little consequence. There was nothing special about Him. And so they missed an opportunity of an eternal lifetime — to meet the Son of God.

We, too, can miss Him when we play the same game. It might be the priest celebrant, the choir, the church building, the other people present, or just about anything else one can imagine — all or any keeping us from "getting" anything out of the Mass.

Being a critic of the Mass has become somewhat of a hobby in the post-Vatican II Church. There are books devoted to identifying whether your priest is celebrating a valid Mass and whom to report him to if he is not. Recently, a priest who writes a question-and-answer column about Catholic issues told me that the majority of questions he receives every month request an answer to whether various practices are allowed. Nine out of ten are allowed, the priest added. In other words, a lot of people are wasting their time policing the way their parish priest says Mass or the way some other minister fulfills a function at Mass.

These attempts at liturgical purity only lead to the worshiper becoming a spectator or a critic. It is a grave temptation that keeps us from fully receiving Christ!

Spectators surrounded our Lord both during His ministry and while He hung upon the cross. Only those who reached out in faith and touched His cloak received the grace that flowed from Him. We, too, will not receive the innumerable graces that can be ours if we come to the Holy Sacrifice of the Mass only looking for evidence of His absence.

The shortcomings of liturgy are always present if we look hard enough. I have heard the most orthodox priests complain about being the victims of witch-hunting purists. If someone is doing something wrong, by all means work to correct the problem, but do not allow yourself to be distracted from the gifts God wishes to bestow upon you during the sacred act of the Mass.

SP 2: YOUR CHEST IS BLOCKED

Some of us block our hearts to our Lord when we show up at Mass filled with desires that we think and believe have nothing to do with God. If that's the case, we're only nominally showing up, because our thoughts are someplace else. Sometimes we are preoccupied with our treasures, a person, or ourselves. We have not yet realized that at the root of whatever our heart desires is communion with God.

Saint Augustine, who spent his youth seeking his heart's desires, finally realized this when he said that "our hearts are restless until they rest in thee" — the "thee" referring to God.

There is a point in every Mass at which we can bring our desires to God. But because many of us do not see the connection, we miss it. There is also a time to hear what the Word of God has to say about our desires. It is not necessary to ignore these desires that weigh upon our hearts, but to bring them to God in the context of what God is saying to us during Mass.

Think of those in the Gospels who came face-to-face with our Lord, but let pass an opportunity to bring their needs and desires before the very creator of the universe. They stood in the presence of the God who could answer all of their prayers, and yet because they were focused on something or someone else, they missed that opportunity!

Whatever it is that we are worried about during Mass, we should avail ourselves of the Lord's Presence. Refusing to recognize Him as the source of all being, we are no different from those who, after meeting our Lord, told Him, "Let me first go and bury my father" (Luke 9:59). In other words, "I like what you're saying, but I have something more important to do right now!"

We should not deny our hearts' desires, but we should bring them to God and allow Him to reveal what it is we truly desire.

OPPORTUNITY FOR SPIRITUAL GROWTH

If you find your mind wandering during Mass, take a moment to focus on what has your attention. Is there something God might be asking you to pay attention to in your life? Does it refer to an area of your life that you are keeping from God? Present God with your heart's desires and ask Him for the wisdom to understand what they mean.

When the woman with the hemorrhage reached out in a crowd and touched Jesus, she was healed (Matthew 9:20-23). This was what she truly desired, and by bringing it to Jesus, her prayer was answered beyond her wildest dreams.

When we bring our hearts to Mass and open them up to our Lord, He will fill them with a treasure that can neither rust nor be eaten by moths, a treasure that satisfies our desires.

SP 3: YOUR WHOLE BODY IS BLOCKED

There is a final group who may be reading this in a bookstore, who get nothing out of the Mass because they don't set foot inside a church. I have a special love for and understanding of your plight because of someone I know who was like you for many years.

He was a man who taught me much about the Mass, although he himself did not go. He would point to the sun in the sky and tell me it was like the Sacred Host held aloft by the priest during Mass, a constant reminder of the Son of God who looked over all of creation.

I often asked him why he himself did not go, but he would never answer me. Someone else told me the reason. People had made fun of the way he dressed and had made him feel unworthy to be there.

Later in his life he returned, always dressed in a suit at a time when most were dressed rather haphazardly. He made his confession, and he received our Lord regularly in the final years of his life on this earth.

I hope you, too, will return, ignoring the modern-day Pharisees or anyone else who has kept or is keeping you from Jesus. If you have sins you are ashamed of, confess them, be forgiven, and return to the Lord, receiving His Body and Blood in the Blessed Sacrament.

OPPORTUNITY FOR SPIRITUAL GROWTH

What do you really believe in? Has something replaced God in your life? Are there sins you have committed that you feel are keeping you from God?

Jesus Christ reveals how much God loves us. God is rich in mercy and wishes for all to be saved. Think about the mercy Jesus bestowed on the sinners He encountered while He walked the earth. See our Lord driving out anything that is keeping you from worshiping Him in the same way that He cleansed the temple in Jerusalem of the moneychangers.

Ask Him to reveal His mercy to you, and open your soul to God.

The centurion whose servant was ill told our Lord that he was not worthy for Him to come under his roof (Luke 7:6). None of us is worthy. We are all sinners. If you are convinced of your sinfulness, congratulations — our Lord died for us while we were still sinners.

Our Lord often dined with sinners and was publicly scorned for doing so. Today is no different. Every church is filled with sinners who ask His forgiveness and learn from Him the way to eternal life. We are His children and He cares for us in the same way that any good parent would care for his child. The Psalmist said, "For God alone my soul waits in silence; from him comes my salvation. He only is my rock and my salvation, my fortress" (Psalm 62:1-2).

There is another way to block your entire body from the Lord and yet be present in the church and that is by refusing to truly die to yourself. Saint Paul, writing about the Christian life, said, "The body is not meant for immorality, but for the Lord, and the Lord for the body" (1 Corinthians 6:13). Those of us who enter the church must realize that conversion is an ongoing process, and that we must constantly measure ourselves against the ideal of the Gospel. Sadly, sometimes we fall into the trap of acting as though the way we live our lives has nothing to do with the faith we profess.

What every one of us longs for is the God that Jesus Christ has fully revealed to us. We will come to hear of Him in the Scriptures, and we will come to recognize Him in the Breaking of the Bread at Mass. Do not entrust your soul to anyone else, but open yourself to the many graces that God wishes to bestow upon you!

1

—— How to Enter the Church ——

CONTENTS OF THIS CHAPTER

- The Origin of the Mass
- Our Response
- Opening the Door
- Holy Water
- Blessing Yourself
- Genuflecting vs. Bowing
- Kneeling or Sitting
- Becoming Aware of God's Presence
- Meditation — "... Jesus himself drew near and went with them."

THE ORIGIN OF THE MASS

Almost two thousand years ago, on the night before He died, Jesus of Nazareth celebrated the Passover meal with His disciples. They gathered in an upper room in Jerusalem. Scripture tells us that at the end of the meal, Jesus suddenly departed from the well-known ritual. He took bread into His hands, said a blessing over it, then broke it as His disciples watched.

Then Jesus gave the fragments to them, saying, "Take, eat; this is my body" (Matthew 26:26).

We can only wonder what the disciples thought as they received this bread He declared to be His Body. Did the fragments remind them of the multiplication of the loaves? Did it remind them of the time they had forgotten to bring bread and Jesus had told them He was the Bread of Life? Only Luke's Gospel records a response to these words, telling us that a dispute broke out among them (cf. Luke 22-24).

Jesus then took a cup filled with wine and gave thanks to God for its contents. Then looking at those in His Presence, He said to them, "This cup which is poured out for you is the new covenant of my blood" (Luke 22:20). "Do this, as often as you drink it, in remembrance of me" (1 Corinthians 11:25).

Jesus declared a "new" covenant between God and humanity. Like the Paschal meal that He celebrated on that night with His disciples, this New Covenant will be celebrated by the followers of Jesus until He comes again. It is this New Covenant that we celebrate each time we come to Mass.

THE FAITH OF THE EARLY CHURCH

"Jesus Christ is the door of the Father, through which enter Abraham and Isaac and Jacob and the Prophets and the Apostles and the Church."

— Saint Ignatius of Antioch, A.D. 110

OUR RESPONSE

What is our response to the command of Jesus? Jesus' "body," His "blood," "Do this ... in remembrance of me"?

Do we realize that our very existence depends upon our response?

Walking toward the church door we are mindful that, as hard as it is sometimes to get to that door, our very life depends upon what waits for us behind the walls of this church — the very Body and Blood of the One who said, "I am the way, and the truth, and the life" (John 14:6).

Without Christ we are as good as dead.

No one thinks much about this anymore. People consider themselves very scientific and sophisticated, but everyone seems to gloss over the fact that our experience tells us that we come into existence in our mother's womb, and when we breathe our last breath, our body immediately starts to decay and we cease to exist. Death is the end ... it is our faith in God that teaches us that there is life after death.

Yes, other things might *seem* more important, and indeed they would be if this life is all there is, but if there is a chance for life after death, then getting to that church door is well worth every effort I can make. In fact, getting through that door is the most important thing I will do in my earthly life.

OPENING THE DOOR

Church doors are often large and cumbersome to open. There is great symbolism in the doors of a church. Sometimes they include frescoes depicting the whole of salvation history on them. In the ancient liturgy (a tradition that still exists in the Eastern Catholic and Orthodox churches), there was a point at which the deacon would call out to the congregation, "The doors, the doors!" The ushers would ensure that the doors had been barred so the uninitiated could not enter or be present to witness the sacred mysteries that were about to unfold. This ancient ritual exists today when we witness the catechumens being dismissed before the recitation of the creed.

— WHAT IS IT?—

 A person who has not been baptized and wishes to join the Catholic Church enters into a period of instruction and formation in the Christian way of life and belief. This process is called the "catechumenate" and the person a "catechumen." Sometimes those who are joining the Catholic Church and have been baptized in another Christian Church also participate in this process. At the Easter Vigil, the catechumens are baptized and confirmed, receive the Holy Eucharist, and become full members of the Christian community.

Your church may or may not have ornate doors, but the symbolism of what the door signifies remains. Sometimes you will see the image of Christ holding a lamb on His shoulders painted or depicted in stained glass over the front doors of a church. This reminds us that Jesus said, "I am the door; if any one enters by me, he will be saved, and will go in and out and find pasture" (John 10:9).

Now it might be good to stop right here. Jesus says that if anyone enters through Him (the door), that person will be saved.

Here is the question you should ask yourself as you approach the door: What is it that Jesus is going to save me from?

So here we encounter the first image of Christ — the door. Someone may open it for us, or we may open it ourselves (again very symbolic of how we can come to the faith in the first place), but we should be mindful that as we pass through this threshold, it is as though we are grasping a life preserver, something that our very existence depends upon.

CATECHISM OF THE CATHOLIC CHURCH

 The *Catechism of the Catholic Church* spells out the state of humanity without Christ — i.e., original sin — by calling to mind what happened to Adam and Eve and to all of their descendants after the fall from grace:

"The harmony in which they found themselves, thanks to original justice, is now destroyed: the control of the soul's spiritual faculties over the body is shattered; the union of man and woman becomes subject to tensions, their relations henceforth marked by lust and domination. Harmony with creation is broken: visible creation has become alien and hostile to man. Because of man, creation is now subject 'to its bondage and decay.' Finally, the consequence explicitly foretold for this disobedience will come true: man will 'return to the ground,' for out of it he was taken. *Death makes its entrance into human history.*" — *CCC*, No. 400

You might wish to read Genesis 3 and reflect on what the *Catechism* teaches about this chapter of the Bible.

HOLY WATER

Near the door or in the center of the space you enter into, you will find one of two sacred items: a holy water font or a baptismal font. The first is a small object, meant to be a miniature holder and reminder of the other.

This water is blessed. It is holy. Ideally, it was blessed at the Easter Vigil for the express purpose of being used in the baptizing of the catechumens. The water then was placed in containers (in the case of holy water fonts) or kept in the baptismal font. In either case, it is appropriate that this water of baptism is the first sacred matter you encounter as you pass through the doors into the church. This water is the price of your admission.

At your baptism you, your parents, or your godparents (if you were baptized as an infant) vowed that you would die to sin and live for Christ. Have you done that? At this moment where is your mind? What are you concerned about? Is it Christ?

HOW TO BLESS YOURSELF AND MAKE THE SIGN OF THE CROSS

To bless yourself, dip the forefingers of your right hand into the blessed water. Bring the same fingers to your forehead, touching it for a second, then move the same hand to your chest, touching it for a second. Move to your left shoulder and touch it with the same hand for a second, then finally over to the right shoulder for a second:

- **As you touch your forehead, say to yourself:** "In the name of the Father ..."

- **As you touch your chest, say to yourself:** "... and of the Son ..."

- **As you touch your left shoulder, say to yourself:** "... and of the Holy ..."

- **As you touch your right shoulder, say to yourself:** "... Spirit. Amen."

You have just blessed yourself by making the sign of the cross with holy water.

BLESSING YOURSELF

This is a manual recalling of your baptism. You were baptized "in the name of the Father, and of the Son, and of the Holy Spirit."

Then the priest or deacon immersed you or poured water over you. Now you bring the water to your body and once again claim that you are Christ's by making His sign over your body with the waters of baptism.

It is an act that can become habitual and at times thoughtless. If this has happened to you, make an effort to once again do this with meaning, recalling the sacred act of your baptism, which forever has marked you as belonging to Christ. Do it with great reverence, thoughtfulness, and gratitude.

GENUFLECTING VS. BOWING

It is necessary in all prayer to be mindful of the Presence of God. In prayer we are talking to some*one*, not some*thing*. Walking into a Catholic Church, we are about to pray the greatest prayer any Christian can pray — the Mass.

What we do before we enter a pew or choose a seat depends on the layout of the church. If the tabernacle, which contains the Blessed Sacrament — the Real Presence of Jesus Christ — is at the front of the church, we genuflect toward our king, honoring Him, before entering the row where we will sit.

HOW TO GENUFLECT OR TO BOW

 Genuflecting is simply lowering ourselves onto the right knee until it touches the floor. At the same time we make the sign of the cross by touching the fingers of our right hand to our forehead, then to our breast, then to our left shoulder and to our right shoulder.

A profound bow is accomplished by bending forward at the waist completely in the direction of the sacred object.

A slight bow of the head is made at the mention of the name of Jesus, the Blessed Virgin Mary, and the saint whose feast day it is.

This is an act of adoration. It should immediately help us to be mindful that we are in the Presence of God. How would we act if someone important were in the room? Well, there is no one more important than the living God!

What should you do if the tabernacle is not in the main body of the church, or if the sanctuary lamp is not lit, signifying that the tabernacle is empty (as is the case on Good Friday and at the beginning of the Easter Vigil Mass)? In such an instance, one should make a profound bow toward the altar, which is another sacred object within the Church that symbolizes Christ.

The bow is an act of reverence toward an object that has deep symbolic meaning, while a genuflection is an act of adoration not toward a symbolic object, but toward the actual Presence of Jesus Christ, the Son of God.

WHAT IS IT?

 ALTAR The sacred table where the Eucharist is celebrated. Sometimes it resembles a table, calling to mind the "banquet"; other times it resembles a tomb, reflecting the early Church's practice of celebrating the Mass on the tombs of the martyrs and calling to mind the entombment of the Lord, who died and rose again from the dead. The Catechism of the Catholic Church refers to the altar as "the Lord's Cross" (No. 1182).

TABERNACLE A box sometimes shaped in the form of a temple, where the Blessed Sacrament (hosts that have been consecrated at a previous Mass) — the Real Presence of our Lord Jesus Christ — is kept.

SANCTUARY LAMP A candle that burns either near the tabernacle or hangs from the ceiling of the church. The lit candle signifies that the tabernacle contains the Blessed Sacrament.

KNEELING OR SITTING

What you do next depends upon the architecture of the church you are in. If there are kneelers you make the sign of the cross and kneel. If there are no kneelers you sit in a prayerful posture with your hands resting on your lap. The posture in either case is one of prayer.

Empty your heart to God. Sometimes it is helpful to pray a few memorized prayers (there are prayers in Appendix I, on Pages 223-226, that you can also pray at this time), but these should always be followed by a real conversation with God. Tell Him all that is on your mind. Do not try to drive out your thoughts as though God could not possibly be interested in them. Your thoughts are an excellent place to invite God into your life.

Reflect on where God is in your life as you kneel or sit there in the church. Do you think about God at all times? Or is this one of those rare occasions?

Try not to distract others, especially if you can see they are trying to pray.

BECOMING AWARE OF GOD'S PRESENCE

Be aware of the Presence of God.

God is everywhere. It is when we come to prayer that we should turn our attention to fostering a deep sense of God's Presence.

Acknowledge God's Presence in the Eucharist. Tell Jesus all of your concerns, and ask Him to be more real to you. Ask Him to help you to feel the reality of His Presence in your midst and to be aware that you will take that presence with you when you leave the church today.

Kneeling and facing the tabernacle is a good way to build an awareness of God's Presence in your life. Your body is cooperating in this act and is helping you to acknowledge that this is not "business as usual," but rather that something important is happening here.

MEDITATION

That very day two of them were going to a village named Emmaus, about seven miles from Jerusalem, and talking with each other about all these things that had happened. While they were talking and discussing together, Jesus himself drew near and went with them. But their eyes were kept from recognizing him.

— Luke 24: 13-16

"... Jesus himself drew near and went with them."

When the Risen Christ first encountered two of His disciples on the road to Emmaus, they did not recognize Him. They were so caught up in their conversation that they barely noticed His Presence when He joined them. But He was there, nonetheless. Almost imperceptibly He joined them and walked with them.

Your mind may be so full when you enter the church that you may arrive at your seat or pew and not even be aware that someone has joined you. The conversations going on in your head may seem like the most important matters at hand, and you may miss out on seeing or coming to know what really is important.

When Jesus drew near the city of Jerusalem, He stopped at a spot on the Mount of Olives where the entire city could be viewed, and He wept. There is a chapel on that spot that exists today, built in the shape of a teardrop. It commemorates the spot where *Dominus Flevit*, "the Lord wept."

Jesus wept there and, as He cried, He spoke: "Would that

even today you knew the things that make for peace! But now they are hid from your eyes. For the days shall come upon you, when your enemies will cast up a bank about you and surround you, and hem you in on every side, and dash you to the ground, you and your children within you, and they will not leave one stone upon another in you; because you did not know the time of your visitation" (Luke 19:42-44).

This is your time of visitation. This is the moment of your encounter with the Lord.

It is not a matter of clearing our minds of all thoughts or of trying to pay attention. No, at this point, when we are preparing ourselves, it is simply a matter of who we will discuss all that is on our minds with — ourselves or God?

The wise person will realize this visitation and make his conversation with God, who deems to make Himself available to His creation.

Hopefully, you have arrived early enough to spend quality time preparing yourself for the great gift you are about to receive. If not, make an effort in the future to arrive in plenty of time to truly prepare yourself for this encounter.

OPPORTUNITY FOR SPIRITUAL GROWTH

Try to arrive early for Mass so that you will have time to collect yourself and to spend some quality time in personal prayer before the communal prayer of the Mass begins.

2

How to Celebrate the Opening Rites

CONTENTS OF THIS CHAPTER

- **The Opening Hymn**
- **The Procession**
- **The Sign of the Cross and the Greeting**
- **Meditation — " 'What is this conversation ...?' "**

THE OPENING HYMN

We have arrived as individuals, and indeed up to this point we have prayed as individuals. All of our thoughts and prayers have been between God and us. But the Mass is a communal prayer, so to help us join with the others who are gathered as the Body of Christ in the Church, we now sing together.

Truly worshiping God requires the death of our ego. Jesus said that no one could be His disciple unless they took up their cross and denied their very self and followed Him. Unfortunately, many of us fail to deny ourselves at this crucial moment of the Mass, refusing to join in the singing of the opening hymn.

We may have our reasons: We can't carry a note (then sing quietly), or we don't like the song (then die to yourself and sing it anyway). *There is no greater obstacle to an experience of God than our refusal to die to ourselves.*

In the same way, we should not sing so loudly as to drown out those around us. The goal of the opening hymn is to bring the Body of Christ together, not to tear it asunder.

As Saint Augustine said, *Cantare amantis est*, "To sing is characteristic of the lover." We give evidence of our love for God by raising our voices in song at the beginning of the Mass.

THE FAITH OF THE EARLY CHURCH

"On the day we call the day of the sun, all who dwell in the city or country gather in the same place."

— Saint Justin Martyr, A.D. 155

THE PROCESSION

While the opening hymn is being sung, those with an official ministry to perform enter the church in a solemn procession. A server bearing incense may come first. Next is the cross bearer holding aloft the sign of our salvation, with two altar servers holding candles on either side. If there are other servers, they follow the cross bearer. If there are concelebrants, they come next. A deacon or lector carries the Book of the Gospels overhead. Last is

---

CATECHISM OF THE CATHOLIC CHURCH

 There is a temptation to consider the Mass as something that the priest or bishop celebrates and we observe. We should avoid that temptation! The *Catechism of the Catholic Church* says about the celebration of the Mass:

"It is the whole *community*, the Body of Christ united with its Head, that celebrates." — *CCC*, No. 1140

That is not to say that everyone has the same role in the celebration, though. The *Catechism* also points out that:

"Certain members are called by God, in and through the Church, to a special service of the community. These servants are chosen and consecrated by the sacrament of Holy Orders, by which the Holy Spirit enables them to act in the person of Christ the head, for the service of all the members of the Church." — *CCC*, No. 1142

And:

"Servers, readers, commentators, and members of the choir also exercise a genuine liturgical function." — *CCC*, No. 1143

The *Compendium of the Catechism of the Catholic Church* sums this up, saying:

"The baptized offer themselves in spiritual sacrifice; the ordained ministers celebrate according to the Order they received for the service of all the members of the Church; the bishops and priests act in the Person of Christ the Head." — *Compendium*, No. 235

WHO ARE THEY?

READER(S) The person(s) who will proclaim the First and Second Readings from the **LECTIONARY** (a book that contains selections of Sacred Scripture arranged for use in the Mass) to the congregation.

SERVER A person who assists the celebrant of the Mass.

DEACON An ordained man who may proclaim the Gospel and assist the celebrant at the altar.

CONCELEBRANT A priest who is not the principle celebrant.

CELEBRANT A priest or bishop who is presiding at the Mass.

the presider of the liturgy, a priest or bishop. If there are two deacons, one will be with the Mass celebrant.

The procession allows the presider of the liturgy and the other ministers to enter the church in an orderly way.

Once they arrive at the sanctuary of the church, together they will make a solemn bow toward the altar. The deacon and priest will go to the altar and venerate it by kissing it. Remember, the altar is a symbol of Christ.

While all of this is going on, the opening hymn continues. Sometimes if the church is large and the procession is long, the singing may go on for some time. Do not be distracted by this, but rather realize that all of this is helping you to let go of yourself and to be open to God. Consider thoughts of refusing to sing or of stopping as a temptation to sin.

THE SIGN OF THE CROSS AND THE GREETING

The priest and, with him, the entire congregation once again make the sign of the cross. The sign of the cross reminds us of our

"By the *sign of the cross* all magic ceases; all incantations are powerless; every idol is abandoned and deserted; all irrational voluptuousness is quelled; and each one looks up from earth to heaven." — Saint Athanasius *(De Incarn. Verbi, t.1)*

"Let none be weary: take up arms against adversaries in the cause of the cross itself: set up faith of the cross as a trophy against the gainsayers. For when you are about to dispute with unbelievers concerning the cross of Christ, first make with your right hand the *sign of the cross* of Christ, and the gainsayer will be dumb. Be not ashamed to confess the cross."

— Saint Cyril of Jerusalem *(Catech. Xiii. n. 22)*

"Keep the door of your heart shut, and frequently defend your forehead with the *sign (seal) of the cross,* lest the exterminator of Egypt find some (unguarded) spot in you." — Saint Jerome *(Ep. Cxxx. n. 9)*

(emphasis added)

Savior, Jesus Christ, and how He died for us on the wood of the cross. It is a sign of God's love for us, that while we were sinners, He sent His Son to save us from our sin. We remind ourselves that Jesus by His cross has overcome the powers of sin and death.

What we did by ourselves upon entering the church, we now do with everyone gathered in the church. We are no longer alone, but with others who believe in and trust God in the same way we do. Every part of the Mass is a reminder that we are not alone — God is with us, and so are our fellow believers.

Next, in the words of Saint Paul the Apostle, the priest greets us. If a bishop presides, he will use the words of Jesus to greet us (see Page 54). Both of these were standard greetings in Jesus' day, very much like "Good morning" or "Hello" is for us today. Our reply to the priest or bishop also comes from Scripture. Both in 2 Timothy 4:22, "The Lord be with your spirit," and in Galatians 6:18, "The grace of our Lord Jesus Christ be with your spirit, brethren," we have the origin of how we respond to the greeting of the celebrant. Although this response was used in the time of Jesus as a typical response — as one might say, "You too," today — at an early point the Church restricted the use of "and with your spirit" to the ordained. It came to be a way of recognizing the presence of the Holy Spirit, conferred on the priest at ordination, present at this Mass, working through the priest.

There are many greetings throughout the Mass. All of them derive from the Scriptures, and knowing where they are from helps us appreciate the part of the Mass we are celebrating.

WHERE IS IT IN SCRIPTURE?

THE SIGN OF THE CROSS

"Go therefore and make disciples of all nations, baptizing them *in the name of the Father and of the Son and of the Holy Spirit.*" — Matthew 28:19 *(emphasis added)*

THE GREETINGS

A priest celebrant greets us with:

"The grace of the Lord Jesus Christ and the love of God and the fellowship of the Holy Spirit be with you all." — 2 Corinthians 13:14

"Grace to you and peace from God our Father and the Lord Jesus Christ." — 1 Corinthians 1:3

"The Lᴏʀᴅ be with you!" — Ruth 2:4

A bishop celebrant greets us with the words of Jesus:

"Peace be with you." — John 20:26

The greeting a bishop uses at Mass, "Peace be with you," contains the words that the Risen Lord Jesus used when He appeared before His apostles in the locked upper room. They call to mind that this Jesus, whose cross we have just witnessed in procession, is not dead, but alive. They remind us that after Jesus said these words, He showed them the wounds in His hands and in His feet. Jesus is alive!

The words that a priest uses are from the Book of Ruth and Saint Paul's letters. They communicate the same message of peace that comes from God the Father and Jesus.

Both greetings invoke peace upon us. Have you ever wondered why? Why should a greeting of "Peace" be the way in which the Mass begins?

Again, think about your state of mind. What are you thinking about? The apostles were locked in a room for fear of the authorities who had crucified Jesus. Often we can be locked in our own little room with a thousand dreads.

Some will fear their sins ...

Some will fear their personal situation at the time ...

Some will fear upcoming events ...

Some will be preoccupied with the past ...

Listen to the greeting of peace and accept it into the deepest core of your being.

MEDITATION

And [Jesus] said to them, "What is this conversation which you are holding with each other as you walk?"

— Luke 24:17

" 'What is this conversation ...?' "

When Jesus encountered the disciples on the road to Emmaus, He asked them what they were discussing as they made their way.

They looked at Him as they would a stranger. They did not recognize Him; they did not know who He was, but because they were disciples, they knew they should welcome the stranger as Christ Himself (see Matthew 25:35).

Gathered in this church, you are surrounded by people. Some you may know; many you do not. Do you welcome all in attendance as Christ Himself?

Jesus told His disciples that they were not to judge.

It is hard to accept peace in our hearts when our hearts are troubled.

What is on your mind? How does the peace of God filter into your consciousness? What conversations are you having inside your head? Do they revolve around the people sitting near you? Your child crying in the pew next to you? The musicians? The priest?

There are so many things that can keep us from recognizing the Presence of God all around us. At this moment He is there where you are, and He wants to hear what you have to say. Tell Him.

OPPORTUNITY FOR SPIRITUAL GROWTH

- Acknowledge God as God, and let go of all the obstacles.

- Ask Him for the grace to let go of your judgments so you will not miss Him in the moment of His visitation.

- Ask Him to help you to not ignore anything He places in your path.

3

How to Celebrate the Penitential Rite

CONTENTS OF THIS CHAPTER

- **Preparation**
- **Silence**
- **The *Confiteor***
- **Striking Our Breast**
- **Pray for Me**
- **Other Options**
- **May Almighty God Forgive You!**
- **Lord, Have Mercy (*Kyrie*)**
- **Meditation — "... we had hoped ..."**

PREPARATION

The Mass continues with the Penitential Rite. The priest may begin this rite by using words that are part of the ritual, or he may choose to invite us to look at our sins in his own words, drawing from the Scripture Readings of the day.

The priest refers to the Mass we are attending as "sacred mysteries." What we are about to witness is beyond our senses, and to prepare ourselves to truly experience these sacred mysteries, we must divest ourselves of our ego. Rereading "How to Get Something Out of Mass" (see Pages 29-36) may be helpful for some at this point. What is it that I need to let go of to truly celebrate the sacred act of God coming into our midst?

In the past forty years there has been a general loss of consciousness of sin. So it might be good to define what sin is. Sin is anything that "breaks my relationship with God." Anything that I choose other than God or God's will for me is sin. Acknowledging that we have sinned is an important starting point if we are to enter into our need for salvation.

Jesus told a parable of two men praying in the temple. One man was very religious and felt that he was perfect, so he prayed to God and thanked Him for not making him like the other. The other man, meanwhile, stood off at a distance, fearing God and declaring himself a sinner in dire need of God's mercy (cf. Luke 18:10-14). Jesus praised the second man's prayer.

We delude ourselves if we think we have no need of God. Without God we would cease to exist this very minute. Yet do we live our lives constantly thanking Him, entreating Him for help? Many times our greatest sin is our feeling of self-sufficiency.

Saint Thérèse of Lisieux compared our situation to that of a baby sitting at the foot of a staircase with God, our Father, standing at the top bidding us to come up. The baby wants to climb the steps to meet the Father, but is incapable of doing so. The Father, looking with love on His small child, will soon come down and bring the baby to the top with Him. At how many moments in our spiritual lives have we looked to the Father for help in our helplessness?

It is important to make use of this part of the Mass that focuses on our sinfulness, to foster a deep sense of our need for God. While some may have been overly sensitive to sin in the past and never availed themselves of God's love and mercy, today many fail to be aware of the need they have for forgiveness.

Are there people you are estranged from? Jesus told His disciples that if they realized they had something against a brother on their way to worship God, they should go and be reconciled to their brother first, then bring their brother to the altar to worship God together.

Saint Ignatius of Loyola referred to sin as a disordered attachment. We place our hope and trust in some created person or thing in a way that is disordered. Why is it disordered? Because God alone can give us what we truly need in life.

Perhaps this is the way to capture a sense of sin in your life: What dominates your thoughts? What do you think will make you happy? If you answer anything other than God to these questions, it could be a disordered attachment.

Call to mind these things that fill your mind.

SILENCE

A period of silence follows. We are given time to think and reflect.

It is interesting that along with a declined sense of sin, people also have grown uncomfortable with silence. We live in a world where we are bombarded with noise in almost every waking moment. But in silence, God speaks to us.

"Be still, and know that I am God" (Psalm 46:10).

Noise often keeps us from hearing God's pleas spoken to our hearts. Use these seconds to allow God to show you what He wishes for you.

HOW TO BE SILENT

Silence is more than not speaking. It is also listening. Be attentive to the quiet. Try to release any thoughts as they come. Open yourself to God's Presence.

THE CONFITEOR

Confiteor is a Latin word that means "I confess," the first words of the prayer that we now say together. This is a public confession. There are only sinners present in the church today. Everyone — priest, deacon, and all gathered — say the words together.

This prayer is directed not only to God but also to everyone present, including the people around us. We acknowledge our acts of separation have occurred through our own fault, emphasizing this by striking our breast (see Page 63). We have sinned in our minds, in our hearts, in our actions and, worst of all, in what we have not done. Our confession is an admission that we are in desperate need of a savior. We open our hearts with this general confession to all gathered that we, like them, are in need of someone to rescue us from our plight. The wages of sin, our sin, is death.

Our sins have other consequences than those felt in the here and now. Our sins create discord, sow fear, and cause great pain. They create a living hell for those around us and even in us. Not only do we need a savior who can rescue us, we also need a savior who can empower us to live our lives differently.

STRIKING OUR BREAST

At the words "through my fault," we strike our breast. Why?

In the ancient world, striking one's breast was a sign of mourning.

At Jesus' death on the cross, the Gospel of Luke recounts that the crowd returned to their homes "beating their breasts" (Luke 23:48). Zechariah the prophet had prophesied that the inhabitants of Jerusalem would do this when he said, "When they look on him whom they have pierced, they shall mourn for him, as one mourns for an only child" (Zechariah 12:10).

Our sins are our death warrant. We beat our breast as we declare our sinfulness in the *Confiteor* in imitation of the tax collector who "standing far off, would not even lift up his eyes to heaven, but beat his breast, saying, 'God, be merciful to me a sinner' " (Luke 18:13).

HOW TO BEAT YOUR BREAST

To beat your breast, make a fist with your right hand and bring it to your chest, and strike it.

One should do this for symbolism rather than for show.

You may notice that during the celebration of the Mass some people strike their breasts at other times. Before the Mass was reformed in the 1960s, people would strike their breasts whenever acknowledging their sinfulness in the course of the liturgy. This is no longer necessary, though.

PRAY FOR ME

We call upon the Blessed Virgin Mary, all the angels and saints in heaven, and the people in our midst (our brothers and sisters in Christ) to pray to God for us.

Stop and think about this for a moment. The ancient belief of the Church is that when we gather to pray as a Church, the group that gathers is more than meets the eye. Literally, heaven comes down to this spot, and we are joined by all of its inhabitants — the angels and all the saints. Most Catholic churches have art that symbolizes the presence of these others by statues and painted images. As we ask them to join our prayer, we should be mindful of the purity of their prayers — my neighbor might think for a second to pray for me, but surely if I ask the Mother of God, the saints, and the angels to pray for me, they will do so incessantly.

In a materialistic world, we tend to forget that there is more to the world than meets the eye. We acknowledge the unseen in the signals sent to our cell phones or other wireless devices, but fail many times to call upon the much more powerful force and certainly time-tested power of God's angels and saints.

Give thought to what you are asking the Blessed Virgin Mary, the angels, and the saints to do. Also give thought to what the people gathered with you and the priest are asking you to do and do it. Ask God to hear their prayers!

OTHER OPTIONS

The priest has other options in celebrating this Penitential Rite. It is perfectly legitimate to use these other, shorter options. The purpose is the same: to declare our sinfulness before God and each other and to implore the Lord for His forgiveness and mercy.

These other options are all drawn from Scripture. The second option's first response comes from Baruch 3:2, "Hear, O Lord, and have mercy, for we have sinned before thee," and the second response is taken from Psalm 85:7, "Show us thy steadfast love, O LORD, and grant us thy salvation." The third option for the Penitential Rite is based on Isaiah 61, where the mission of the Messiah is laid out to bring good news to those in bondage. The second declaration of the priest comes from Matthew 9:13: " 'I desire mercy, and not sacrifice.' For I came not to call the righteous, but sinners." The third declaration of the priest is based on Romans 8:34: "Is it Christ Jesus, who died, yes, who was raised from the dead, who is at the right hand of God, who indeed intercedes for us?"

MAY ALMIGHTY GOD FORGIVE YOU!

At the end of the *Confiteor* or one of the other options, the priest prays a prayer of absolution. This is a general prayer of absolution; it does not have the power to forgive us of mortal sins in the way that the prayer of absolution does in the Sacrament of Penance. We should celebrate the Sacrament of Penance if we have serious sin to confess. But in a general way, it reminds us that God has given the Church the power to heal the rift that existed between creation and God before the salvific act of Jesus Christ on the cross.

Bowing your head as the priest says this prayer is one way to accept the mercy of God that is given by the Church through the merits of Jesus Christ. Open your heart to this gift.

LORD, HAVE MERCY *(KYRIE)*

Saint Paul said that it is only in the Spirit that we can acknowledge that Jesus Christ is Lord. In praying the *Kyrie* (Greek for "Lord"), we are acknowledging that Jesus is Lord. When the ancient Jews would come across the sacred name of God in the Scriptures, they were forbidden to say His name. Only the high

- In Matthew 9:27-30, two blind men follow Jesus and cry out, *"Have mercy on us, Son of David."* **After asking them if they have faith, Jesus heals them of their blindness.**

- In Matthew 15:22-28, a Canaanite woman cries out to Jesus, *"Have mercy on me, O Lord,* Son of David; my daughter is severely possessed by a demon." **Again, Jesus tests the woman's faith, then heals her daughter.**

- In Mark 10:46-52, Bartimaeus, a blind beggar, cries out to Jesus, "Jesus, Son of David, *have mercy on me!"* **Jesus asks the man what he wants, and Bartimaeus asks for his sight. Jesus heals him of his blindness.** *(emphasis added)*

priest could intone the name once a year. So what did the Jewish people do? Whenever they would come upon the name of God, they would say "Lord."

So in this prayer we pray to Jesus as God and ask Him for His forgiveness for our sins. At times in the history of the Mass, the threefold repetition of "Lord, have mercy" has been a way of asking the Triune God for mercy — the first time we said "Lord, have mercy" we were invoking the Father, the "Christ, have mercy" referred to the Son, and the final "Lord, have mercy" referred to the Holy Spirit. Older Catholics will also remember that each invocation was said three times instead of two times, as it is now. The current meaning of the "Lord, …" "Christ, …" and "Lord, …" all refer to Jesus.

If the prayer is prayed as *Kyrie, eleison* and *Christe, eleison,* it is the remnants of an ancient prayer in Greek. Because the New Testament was written in Greek, here we are praying in the language of the early Church.

MEDITATION

And they stood still, looking sad. Then one of them, named Cleopas, answered him, "Are you the only visitor to Jerusalem who does not know the things that have happened there in these days?" And he said to them, "What things?" And they said to him, "Concerning Jesus of Nazareth, who was a prophet mighty in deed and word before God and all the people, and how our chief priests and rulers delivered him up to be condemned to death, and crucified him. But we had hoped that he was the one to redeem Israel."

— Luke 24: 17-21

"… we had hoped …"

The disciples on the road to Emmaus told the "visitor" that they "had hoped" that Jesus would "redeem Israel." Of course, we who read the biblical account know that it is the Risen Lord that they are telling this to, but they do not know Him. Their sight is blinded by "their vision." We may smile at their naiveté, but are we any different?

We, too, can be blinded to our Lord's Presence in our midst. It can happen at Mass. We easily become distracted because things are not as we had hoped. We carry within ourselves our own version of what "we hope" will redeem us.

What scandalized the disciples on the road to Emmaus was what the Lord Jesus had suffered at the hands of men. Here was the Lord, mighty in word and deed, who had been handed over by the religious and political leaders of the day, condemned to death, and publicly executed like a common criminal. This was clearly not what they had expected, again because they had their own "idea" of how God should save them.

Jesus never tired of telling His disciples that God's way is not the way of humans. Yet we still forget. We are blinded by our own view of how we think God should act in our lives. We put our plan, our will, before His.

When Jesus was nailed to the cross, He prayed a simple but powerful prayer: "Father, forgive them; for they know not what they do" (Luke 23:34). We can open ourselves up to a powerful encounter with God at this celebration of the Mass if we admit that without the help of God we do not know what we are doing. We are sinners, our intellect is clouded; we see but indistinctly.

Like the blind men on the side of the road, we need the Lord to heal our blindness so that we, too, might recognize Him: "Lord, have mercy on us!"

OPPORTUNITY FOR SPIRITUAL GROWTH

Imagine if you lost everyone close to you tomorrow.

- **Who would you turn to?**

- **What if you were told that you had only a few hours to live?**

- **What would be important at that moment?**

Ask God for the wisdom to place everything in the correct order in your life right now.

4

How to Sing the Gloria

CONTENTS OF THIS CHAPTER

- *Gloria in Excelsis*
- When the Gloria Is Omitted
- The Song of the Angels
- What Is the "Glory" of God?
- Putting God First
- Meditation — "... a vision of angels ..."

GLORIA IN EXCELSIS

Confident that the Lord will forgive us our sins, we now sing out, giving praise to God in imitation of the angels in heaven. This prayer of the Mass is actually an ancient hymn with three parts. The first part is the song that the shepherds heard sung by the heavenly choir of angels at the birth of Christ. The second part praises God by recalling all of His attributes. The third part prays to Jesus, asking Him to save us from our sins.

After calling to mind our sinfulness both in the *Confiteor* and the *Kyrie,* we now call to mind the Incarnation of God. This is a prayer to God the Father, reminding Him that the Church gathered in this building is the incarnate Body of His Son. To do this we sing a Christmas song ... the song the angels sang to the shepherds in Bethlehem.

Monsignor Ronald Knox, in a book called *The Mass in Slow Motion*, written in 1949, spoke of the Gloria as a time to cheer us up after groveling in the first part of the Mass. In case we get too down on ourselves, this prayer is a means to take the focus away from us and to turn it again toward God; giving God praise for sending His Son to save us from our sinful plight. But as Monsignor Knox also points out, there are some times when we wish to "grovel" a bit longer than usual, so the Gloria is omitted during Sundays in Advent and Lent.

WHEN THE GLORIA IS OMITTED

What should we think of when the Gloria is omitted during Advent and Lent? If you are a lifelong Catholic, it may seem awkward when we don't sing the Gloria. This is the power of ritual. We get used to the "sameness" of the Mass, and it disturbs us when there is a break in the ritual. We should pause to reflect during the awkwardness of the seasons of Advent and Lent on why we are not praising God for sending His Son.

During Advent we are "awaiting" the coming of the Lord. The omission of the Gloria, a song that recalls the Lord's First Coming, gives us pause during this season to think of what is missing. It puts us into that time before the Lord's First Coming when, without Him, humanity was stuck in its sinfulness. We listen to the announcements of His coming in the Readings with great anticipation. It also predisposes us to pray for His Second Coming. Ultimately, it prepares us to joyfully sing the Gloria on Christmas when we celebrate the Lord's coming.

During Lent, the focus is different. We do wish to "grovel" a bit longer. It begins with the imposition of ashes on our foreheads on Ash Wednesday, when we are reminded of Adam and Eve's fault — "Remember, you are dust, and to dust you will return." We are called to meditate on what our lives would be like if Christ did not come to save us. It helps, then, to again encounter the absence of the Gloria, which reminds us that Christ has come. It allows us to wallow a bit in our sins, but only to more fully experience what God has done for us in sending His Son, who moves toward Jerusalem to suffer and die for our sins. Fittingly, at the beginning of the Easter Triduum (literally the "three-day festival of Easter") on Holy Thursday, bells will ring joyfully as we sing the Gloria at the end of our long fast!

THE SONG OF THE ANGELS

In the Book of Revelation, John records heaven opening up for him. We get a glimpse of what heaven is like. He tells us that "day and night they never cease to sing, 'Holy, holy, holy, is the Lord God Almighty, who was and is and is to come!' " (Revelation 4:8).

The Mass is a participation in this heavenly liturgy that never ends. And at this point we, too, in this church participate in giving praise to God in the words that the angels used when heaven opened and God became man.

Sometimes the Gloria is referred to as the "great doxology" (a word that means to give glory, praise, or honor to someone). The shorter doxology, which is a combination of belief in the Trinity (God as Father, Son, and Holy Spirit) and Revelation 4:8, is a prayer that most Catholics learn as children, called the Glory Be.

This greater doxology that we now sing is an ancient prayer. The *Apostolic Constitutions,* a document that survives from A.D. 400 (quoted at the beginning of this section), records the Gloria as a morning prayer in use already at the time. In this prayer, we give praise to God by recalling how great He is and worthy of all our worship and devotion.

THE GLORY BE
Glory be to the Father,
and to the Son,
and to the Holy Spirit.
As it was in the beginning,
is now and ever shall be,
world without end.
Amen.

We often think of thanking those on earth who do something nice for us. In a special way we find times throughout the year to thank our mothers and fathers for bringing us into this world and raising us. We send thank-you cards to those who give us gifts. Yet there is no being on earth worthy of more thanks than the one who is our Creator and Lord.

Those in heaven know this, and as the Book of Revelation records, they sing God's praises night and day without ceasing. Here we join them in singing these great words of praise to God.

WHAT IS THE "GLORY" OF GOD?

The word "glory" is used several ways in Scripture.

The most common use of "glory" in Scripture is in reference to the very Presence of God Himself. When Saint Stephen is being stoned to death in the Acts of the Apostles, Luke tells us,

"But he, full of the Holy Spirit, gazed into heaven and saw the glory of God, and Jesus standing at the right hand of God" (Acts 7:55). Here it is clear that "glory" refers to the Presence of God.

When Saint Paul, in his letter to the Corinthians, tells them, "So, whether you eat or drink, or whatever you do, do all to the glory of God" (1 Corinthians 10:31), we have an example of "glory" referring to praise. But there is more to it than that. We tend to thank people who are present, or send them notes of thanks when they are away. Yet for the Christian, God is always present. Therefore, the thanks we give to God at all times is done because the "glory of God" is always before us.

In worshiping God we participate in this "glory" in God's Presence. Our lives are changed. What formerly was done only in the heavens, now because of the coming of Christ is done on earth.

So what the Psalmist proclaims, "The heavens are telling the glory of God; and the firmament proclaims his handiwork" (Psalm 19:1), by singing or saying the Gloria, we on earth, in this church, now also do.

PUTTING GOD FIRST

It is part of our preparation during the Mass to sing this praise to God to rightly put Him first and foremost in our lives. By recounting in the Gloria who God is, then what He has done for us in taking away our sins in Jesus, and finally declaring again that He alone is God, we are making a proclamation that God is our God!

We should reflect on the meaning of this in our lives. Do we place God first? Do we reflect the glory of God in our lives? In other words, do people sense the Presence of God when we are in their midst?

As we sing the Gloria, we should be mindful of God's Presence. In the first covenant, God's glory came down upon the Israelites in the form of a cloud that would descend upon the meeting tent. On the day of Pentecost, when the apostles were gathered in the upper room in Jerusalem, the Holy Spirit came upon them in what looked like tongues of fire. As we raise our minds and hearts to God in this hymn of praise, we should recognize God's Presence in our midst.

We are aware of our need for God, and God has not abandoned us in our need. We should open our hearts to Him and ask Him to make us aware of His Presence in our lives at every moment.

MEDITATION

"Yes, and besides all this, it is now the third day since this happened. Moreover, some women of our company amazed us. They were at the tomb early in the morning and did not find his body; and they came back saying that they had even seen a vision of angels, who said that he was alive. Some of those who were with us went to the tomb, and found it just as the women had said; but him they did not see."

— Luke 24:21-24

"... a vision of angels ..."

The Gospel of Luke begins and ends with a "vision of angels." First, there is the appearance of the Archangel Gabriel to Zechariah and Mary. When Mary later visits Zechariah and Elizabeth, she proclaims that God "has shown strength with his arm, he has scattered the proud in the imagination of their hearts, he has put down the mighty from their thrones, and exalted those of low degree; he has filled the hungry with good things, and the rich he has sent empty away" (Luke 1:51-53). Zechariah, at the birth of John, prophesies that "the day shall dawn upon us from on high to give light to those who sit in darkness and in the shadow of death, to guide our feet into the way of peace" (Luke 1:78-79).

There is a common theme hinted at in both of these canticles — the lowly understand a message that those in power totally miss, hunger is filled, and those who sit in darkness are given light. These precede another vision of angels. In Luke 2:8, immediately following the birth of Jesus, we read about shepherds keeping "night watch" over their flocks. The shepherds are literally a people "who sit in darkness," but who have an experience of light: "The glory of the Lord shone around them" (Luke 2:9).

OPPORTUNITY FOR SPIRITUAL GROWTH

Imagine the most joyful event in your life. Try to recapture that mood as you sing along, giving glory to God!

What is the message given to the shepherds? "Be not afraid; for behold, I bring you good news of a great joy which will come to all the people; for to you is born this day in the city of David a Savior, who is Christ the Lord. And this will be a sign for you: you will find a babe wrapped in swaddling cloths and lying in a manger" (Luke 2:10-12).

We may be too overly familiar with this Christmas story to notice what it might be telling us. What exactly is a sign? It is not an end in and of itself but rather something that points to a greater reality. What is the sign the shepherds are told they will witness? They are told that they will find a "babe wrapped in swaddling cloths and lying in a manger." A manger is a feeding box for animals. We are told that it is a "sign," and that what the shepherds witness points to something beyond the experience of the birth of Christ to something else.

When the angels leave, the shepherds say, "Let us go over to Bethlehem and see this thing that has happened, which the Lord has made known to us" (Luke 2:15). The key word here is "Bethlehem," which literally means "house of bread" — "Let us go over to the *House of Bread* and see this thing that has happened, which the Lord has made known to us."

All of this is how the Gospel of Luke begins, but how does it end? Here the Risen Christ has joined two disciples on the road to Emmaus. They do not recognize Him, and here they tell Him about a "vision of angels" (Luke 24:23) that the women who came to the tomb have reported to them. In response to this, Jesus opens the Scriptures to them. They invite Him to stay with them. He takes bread, says the blessing, breaks it, gives it to them, and then physically vanishes from their site. Luke tells us quite blatantly, for the really dense reader, that they recognized Him in the "breaking of the bread" (Luke 24:35).

Where are we to find Jesus this day? In the bread that is broken in the Eucharist! So at Mass we sing the Gloria, the message of the angels. It is both a reminder and an invitation for us to encounter the Lord here.

The women who witnessed the empty tomb heard the message of the angels and believed that God had raised Jesus from the dead. They believed that He was alive! The disciple whom Jesus loved looked upon the empty tomb and the wrappings lying there, and he too believed! But the disciples on the road to Emmaus who were joined by the Risen Christ were less sure.

We probably are more like those disciples on the road than we are like the others. We, too, have our doubts. But Jesus is with us, and by singing the song of the angels and joining in the heavenly liturgy, we, like the disciples on the road to Emmaus, can come to recognize His Presence.

The message of the angels is ultimately one of God's Presence in our midst. We are about to experience one of the ways God is present to us in His sacred word as we listen to the proclamation of the Scriptures.

Even if we do not sense His Presence, let us open ourselves up to the possibility as we sing His praises with the angels.

5

How to Say "Amen" to the Opening Prayer

CONTENTS OF THIS CHAPTER

- Let Us Pray
- Silence
- The Collect
- Saying "Amen"

LET US PRAY

The presider of the liturgy now asks us to pray — *Oremus* in Latin. *Oremus* can be translated "Let us ask." It is worth mentioning this because the word we translate as "pray" is often thought to mean something else. Some Christians are uncomfortable with the fact that Catholics pray to various saints. But "pray" does not mean worship or adore. It simply means "to ask," and when Catholics pray to saints they are merely "asking" saints to "ask" God for their intentions.

Here the presider asks us to pray; to ask together as the Body of Christ.

The request may be so familiar to us that we may not pause to reflect on what we are doing at this moment. The very act of petitioning God is an act of faith. First, it is an act of faith that God is listening to us — that He is present. Second, it is an act of faith that He is able to fulfill our petition. Third, it is an act of faith that He wishes to answer our pleas.

As we hear the words "Let us pray," it would be good for us to reflect on God the Father, who desires good things for His children. Jesus told His disciples to "ask," and here we are doing exactly that — we are joining together and "asking" in faith.

SILENCE

Before the presider continues with the prayer that he will pray for all of us, there is silence. This period of silence is given to us as a gift. It gives us time to compose ourselves before God, to truly open our hearts to Him and His Presence.

It is also a time to storm heaven with all of our needs. All that is on our mind should be given to God at this moment. All of the preparatory rites have led to this moment when we let go of all that has hold of us — both the good and the bad. If it is our sinfulness, we offer that to the Lord; if it is our anxieties, we ask Him for His peace; if it is our needs, we ask Him to fulfill them. Whatever is on our mind, we present it all before the Lord.

If we are at peace and nothing fills our minds, we think of those around us and their needs — offering the Father prayers on their behalf. In the silent moment, all of the prayers of the congregation rise from within the congregation. The presider will say a prayer that is meant to "collect" the prayers of the congregation and offer them to God the Father on our behalf.

THE COLLECT

The Latin name for this prayer is *Collecta,* meaning "the collect." In the English translations it is called the "opening prayer," which may strike you as odd, considering we have already been saying a variety of prayers since we entered the church. But this prayer takes all of the prayers that we have offered and formally presents them before God the Father, although there are occasions when the prayer is addressed to Jesus.

We approach God as beggars in great need. The presider, who acts in the person of Christ, does the asking for us. So when God hears the prayer, it is as though He hears His Son asking. If you listen to the words of the prayer, which differ at almost every Mass, you will notice that the elements essentially remain the same.

There are four parts to this prayer. There is the calling upon God (either the Father or the Son), the recalling of some deed God has done, a request, and finally the prayer is made through the mediation of the Son.

SAYING "AMEN"

At the close of the prayer, the congregation replies with an "Amen!" This is a response we give throughout the liturgy and an important part of our participation in the Mass. It is our seal of approval; it is our signature to the request. It is our way of saying that we agree with the prayer made by the presider, and that it is, in fact, our prayer, too.

WHAT DOES IT MEAN?

" 'Amen' in the Hebrew language signifies 'so be it.' "

— Saint Justin Martyr, A.D. 155

It can also mean "truly," as when Jesus says:

"Amen, amen, I say to you ..." — John 6:32 (Douay-Rheims)

It can also refer to Jesus, as in the Book of Revelation:

"The words of the Amen, the faithful and true witness, the beginning of God's creation." — Revelation 3:14

We should listen attentively to the opening prayer and make it our own, so that when we proclaim "Amen" with those around us, we really mean it.

6

How to Understand the Liturgy of the Word

CONTENTS OF THIS CHAPTER

- **The Two Parts of the Mass**
- **The Covenant at Mount Sinai**
- **The New Covenant of Jesus**
- **The Liturgy of the Word**
- **Meditation — "... and slow of heart to believe ..."**

THE TWO PARTS OF THE MASS

The Mass has two main parts: the Liturgy of the Word and the Liturgy of the Eucharist. Some may also remember another pair of terms: the Mass of the Catechumens and the Mass of the Faithful, which were terms often used before Vatican II, when hardly anyone remembered what a catechumen was. (If you have forgotten, go back to Chapter 1.)

Those who were being initiated into the faith in the early Church would gather with the faithful on Sundays and listen to the Scriptures being proclaimed. These Readings from the Bible revealed and proclaimed who God was and what He had done for us. But when the Readings had been proclaimed and the presider of the Mass had given instruction from them, the catechumens — those who had not been baptized — had to leave, thus the Mass of the Catechumens.

If you have catechumens in your parish, you will notice that they leave the church building after the homily. This should give you and those who remain for the rest of the Mass pause to reflect on why you are allowed to stay.

THE COVENANT AT MOUNT SINAI

You may recall that I began Chapter 1 with a retelling of the event of the first Mass, the Last Supper. Jesus told His disciples that His Blood was the Blood of the New Covenant. His sacrifice on the cross, this meal that celebrates our covenant with God, was replacing a covenant that God had made with Moses and the Israelite people in the desert.

If we go back to Exodus 24:7-8 we find the celebration of the covenant that God made with Moses and the Israelites at Sinai. Notice the two parts of this ritual celebration in the Scripture box.

— WHERE IS IT IN SCRIPTURE? —

"Then he took the book of the covenant, and read it in the hearing of the people; and they said, 'All that the Lord has spoken we will do, and we will be obedient.' And Moses took the blood and threw it upon the people, and said, 'Behold the blood of the covenant which the Lord has made with you in accordance with all these words.' "

— Exodus 24:7-8

First, Moses reads the covenant to the people. When he is finished, they are faced with a decision: Will they accept the terms of this covenant? And they do.

Second, Moses, in the words of Scripture, throws the blood of the oxen he had sacrificed to the Lord on the people. As he does, he tells them this is the "blood of the covenant."

THE NEW COVENANT OF JESUS

Now, remember the words of Jesus at the Last Supper. As He gives His disciples the cup filled with wine, He says, "This is the blood of the New Covenant." This is what we are celebrating at Mass.

Notice that the Mass has two parts as well. In the Liturgy of the Word, we listen to Readings from the Bible that tell us of the wonders God has done since the beginning of time until the fullness of time, when He took on our human flesh and walked among us, then sacrificed His life to reconcile us to Himself.

At the end of the Readings, we have a decision to make: Will we give assent to what God is asking of us?

If we do, we say the creed, declaring as the ancient Israelites did that we believe in God and all He has done. This is why catechumens leave before the creed is said. They have not reached the point of giving full assent to the faith yet.

CATHOLIC BELIEFS

On Easter Sunday our act of giving assent to the proclamation of the Readings becomes even more evident when the members of the congregation renew their baptismal vows. The presider asks them point-blank:

Do you reject Satan?
And all his works?
And all his empty promises?
Do you believe in God, the Father Almighty,
    creator of heaven and earth?
Do you believe in Jesus Christ, his only Son, our Lord,
    who was born of the Virgin Mary,
    was crucified, died, and was buried,
    rose from the dead,
    and is now seated at the right hand of the Father?
Do you believe in the Holy Spirit,
    the holy catholic Church, the communion of saints,
    the forgiveness of sins, the resurrection of the body,
    and life everlasting?

The second part of the liturgy celebrates the passion and death of our Lord in the way that He instructed His disciples to do so. It is not a sacrifice of oxen, but the sacrifice of our Lord at Calvary.

Remember the covenant at Sinai? The people had the blood of the oxen thrown upon them after they gave their assent to the Word of God that Moses read to them. With that in mind, and with the words of Jesus that His Blood is the Blood of the New Covenant, reflect on the meaning of this passage of Scripture that details the trial of Jesus before Pilate.

WHERE IS IT IN SCRIPTURE?

"So when Pilate saw that he was gaining nothing, but rather that a riot was beginning, he took water and washed his hands before the crowd, saying, 'I am innocent of this man's blood; see to it yourselves.' And all the people answered, 'His blood be on us and on our children!'"

— Matthew 27:24-25

This passage, which has often been interpreted in an anti-Semitic way to blame the Jewish people for the death of Christ, is actually something very different, if we are familiar with the setting of the covenant at Sinai. We are all present in Pilate's court. Notice the passage says that "all the people answered." This blood that we ask to be upon our heads is the saving Blood of the New Covenant.

In the Liturgy of the Eucharist, we fulfill the command of Christ. We agree to the New Covenant, then receive His Body and Blood to seal the deal with God. The latter chapters of this book will walk us through this part of the Mass.

THE LITURGY OF THE WORD

We now arrive at the part of the Mass called the Liturgy of the Word. We will listen attentively as a reader proclaims the Scripture to us from the ambo. We will sing a psalm, then we will hear another Reading.

We might reflect on Moses leading to the Israelites in the
desert. They did not have books in which to follow along, or mis-
sals. It could be that you do not, either. They did not have a pub-
lic-address system. It could be that your church doesn't, either.
But they recognized that what they were listening to wasn't every-
day banter, but rather something very sacred and holy. We need
to foster within ourselves this same sense of awe for the Word of
God that we hear proclaimed at every Mass.

There are more than a few Catholics who do not know where
to find what they are hearing read at Mass on Sundays. Catholics
often fall prey to the lie that the Catholic Church doesn't allow
its followers to read the Bible. Nothing could be further from the
truth. Most of the prayers and responses of the Mass are taken

directly from Scripture. There is never a celebration of the Mass in which the Bible is not read.

The Readings that we hear in the Liturgy of the Word are all from the Bible. In the next chapters, we will find out from what books of the Scriptures they are taken.

MEDITATION

And [Jesus] said to them, "O foolish men, and slow of heart to believe all that the prophets have spoken! Was it not necessary that the Christ should suffer these things and enter into his glory?"

— Luke 24:25-26

"... and slow of heart to believe ..."

We may feel that if we had walked with Jesus and been taught by Him, we all would have instantly understood everything there is to know about the Christian faith. But clearly, that was not the case for the early disciples of our Lord.

The disciples who encountered Jesus on the road to Emmaus were filled with disappointment because what they had hoped Jesus would be had not come to pass.

We, too, have our ideas of the way God should act in our lives. We think we know what will make us happy, and sometimes we enter the church disappointed that God has not acted in the way we think best.

How did the Son of God react to the disciples who expressed their disappointment in the events they had witnessed in Jerusalem?

He called them foolish.

He called them slow to believe the Scriptures.

He told them all that had happened was necessary.

They were foolish because Jesus had told His disciples time and time again that God's ways were not their ways. They were slow to believe because He had predicted His death and Resurrection, and they had obviously ignored Him. Finally, He told them that what had happened was necessary: Most of us, including the disciples, tend to think of the experiences of our lives as something that could have been otherwise, if only we had acted differently.

As we prepare to listen to the Word of God proclaimed in this church, what are our foolish ideas? Are we slow to believe what we will hear proclaimed in Scripture? Do we spend our time reflecting on the past, which is forever behind us?

We may not recognize the Word of God in our midst.

The disciples on the road to Emmaus still did not, but later they would say, "Did not our hearts burn within us while he talked to us on the road, while he opened to us the scriptures?" (Luke 24:32).

Let us present to our Lord all our worries and cares as we listen to His Word proclaimed now, at this Mass. The Scriptures are "living word." They will always speak to us in a way that nothing else can.

OPPORTUNITY FOR SPIRITUAL GROWTH

An excellent way for us to prepare for the Liturgy of the Word is to repeat the ancient prayer of Jesus' disciples.

Simply say, *"Ma ra na tha,"* **an Aramaic word that means** *"Come Lord,"* **over and over, inviting the Lord to reveal Himself to you in His Word.**

7

How to Listen to the First Reading

CONTENTS OF THIS CHAPTER

- Where Is This Reading Taken From?
- The Old Testament
- A Secret About the First Reading
- Easter Time — A Reading From Acts
- Our Response

WHERE IS THIS READING TAKEN FROM?

The Reading we now hear proclaimed by the reader is from the Holy Bible. The reader proclaims the Reading from the ambo using the Lectionary. A Lectionary is a book used at Mass that contains selections from the Bible that are organized for daily use at the Eucharistic liturgy according to the celebration of that particular day. There are slight modifications — if you opened your Bible to a passage to be read at Mass, you might notice that a passage beginning with "when he ..." is changed to "when Moses ...," for example — so we who are listening to the Reading know who is being talked about. But other than clarifications to help us understand the context, the passage being read is the same, word for word, as what you would find in the Revised New American Bible (for Masses celebrated in English in the United States).

We should give our whole attention to the Word of God. In fact, ideally we will prepare ourselves by reading beforehand the parts of the Bible that are going to be read at Mass. If you have a missal, you can find the Readings by locating the Sunday of the year. Next you will have to determine which "cycle" of Readings the Church is using. (There are three for the Sunday Readings.)

Even though we may have heard what is being proclaimed before, we should ask God to open our hearts to hearing His Word anew. God will speak to our hearts if we truly are open.

THE OLD TESTAMENT

The First Reading is always from the Old Testament, except during the Easter Season (which I will touch upon later in this chapter). When our Lord taught His disciples all that Scripture had proclaimed about Him, He was always talking about what we call the Old Testament.

If you own both a Catholic Bible and a non-Catholic Bible, you may be surprised to find that the Catholic Old Testament is longer than the non-Catholic one. If you have a Jewish Bible, you may find that it only has the first five books of the Bible in it. Catholics have forty-six books in their Old Testament; non-Catholics have thirty-nine books in theirs.

The reason for this disparity dates back to the Reformation. The reformers relied on a list of accepted books of the Old Testament that dates to some ninety years after Christ at the Council of Jamnia (a council of Jewish rabbis), whereas Catholics accept the books that the Jewish people held as inspired during the time of Jesus.

WHAT DOES IT MEAN?

 "Testament" is another name for "covenant." It was Jesus who coined the term "New Covenant." Later Christians referred to the Scriptures that existed before Jesus as the Old Testament — i.e., "Old Covenant" — and the sacred writings after Him the New Testament — i.e., "New Covenant."

Calling the Old Testament the "Old Testament" hasn't been in vogue for some time in educated circles. The preferred term is the "Jewish Scriptures," which is a true enough name for that part of our Bible; the problem is that Jesus was a Jew, as were the early Christians. The New Testament was written by Jews. So to this author it seems rather unfair to call one part of the Bible "Jewish" and ignore the other part's Jewish origin.

The early Christians (and all who have succeeded them) believed that Jesus fulfilled the promises God had made to the Jewish people recorded in the Old Testament and evident in the New Testament. The Gospel of John remarks that at the death of Jesus, "these things took place that the scripture might be fulfilled …" (John 19:36).

A SECRET ABOUT THE FIRST READING

Most Catholics are unaware of a little secret about the First Reading (when it's from the Old Testament). This little fact really isn't a secret, but so few know about it that it might as well be. The First Reading is chosen because it somehow relates to the Gospel Reading of the day.

Every Sunday's First Reading and Gospel have some connection, except during the Easter Season. Listening carefully, one can devise his or her own homily from the connection. Hopefully, the homilist (the preacher) will, too!

CATHOLIC PRACTICES

 On the First Sunday of Lent, Cycle A, the First Reading is taken from the Book of Genesis, Chapter 2, Verses 7-9; and Chapter 3, Verses 1-7. It is the account of Adam and Eve in the Garden of Eden, and Eve's temptation by the serpent. *Adam and Eve succumb to Satan's temptation.*

The Gospel for the same Sunday is taken from the Gospel of Matthew, Chapter 4, Verses 1-11. It is the account of the temptation of Jesus by Satan. *Jesus does not succumb to the temptation of Satan.*

In the example above, you and I can relate to Adam and Eve's failure because we, too, have fallen so often. But Jesus' faithfulness points out to us that although fully human, He is not like us in that His trust in God does not waver in time of temptation.

We should pray that when we receive Him in the Eucharist, His Presence within us will empower us to follow His example, and not that of Adam and Eve.

EASTER TIME — A READING FROM ACTS

Beginning with Easter Sunday, the First Reading is taken from the Acts of the Apostles. This continues until the end of the Easter Season on Pentecost Sunday. During this celebration of the Lord's Resurrection, the proclamation of Acts allows us to focus on what life for Jesus' disciples was like in the early Church.

If we listen carefully to the Readings from this book of the Bible, we will marvel at how the disciples were transformed by the Risen Christ. When they received the Holy Spirit, they began to do the very works that previously had been done only by our Lord. The Acts of the Apostles makes it clear that all Jesus did, He now has empowered His Church to do.

WHERE IS IT IN SCRIPTURE?

Jesus tells His disciples:

"Truly, truly, I say to you, he who believes in me will also do the works that I do; and greater works than these will he do, because I go to the Father." — John 14:12

In the Acts of the Apostles, they experience this:

- **Peter and John heal a crippled beggar (Acts 3:1-10).**
- **The apostles heal the multitudes (Acts 5:12-16).**
- **Philip performs exorcisms and miracles (Acts 8:6-7).**
- **Ananias cures Saul's blindness (Acts 9:17-19).**
- **Peter heals a paralytic (Acts 9:33-34).**
- **Peter raises Tabitha from the dead (Acts 9:36-41).**
- **Barnabas and Paul heal (Acts 14:8-10).**

Read the Acts of the Apostles for many more examples.

The Acts of the Apostles begins in Jerusalem and ends in Rome. In this narrative, we encounter how the early Church became a living witness to Jesus, with each follower becoming "another Christ," sharing in His cross through suffering, even to the point of giving up one's life for the message, but also sharing in His power as great miracles were worked in His name. This witness explains the growth of the early Christian community from a small band of apostles to a Church that numbers over a billion today.

OUR RESPONSE

Whether the First Reading is from the Old Testament or from the Acts of the Apostles in the New Testament, it demands a response from us. The Word of God proclaimed is not left to hang in the air. It is either accepted or ignored by those who hear it.

The Word of God is presented to us with "The Word of the Lord" in the same way that the Eucharist is presented to us with the words "The Body of Christ" and "The Blood of Christ." Just as there is a communion and bond achieved by reception of the Eucharist, so too, in our reception of the Word of God, do we come to truly "know" the Lord. We respond with words from the Bible by saying, "Thanks be to God."

Where is this from? Knowing the answer helps us to meditate on what we mean when we say it.

No matter what the Word of God has set before us, we rejoice because of the grace of Jesus Christ. We give thanks to God as Saint Paul did because we are no longer lost. Through the power of God, made available to us because of what God the Son has done (and is doing during this Mass), God's Holy Spirit can empower us to respond to God's Word not as wretched slaves, but as a freed people who now can fulfill God's commands.

The phase "Thanks be to God" occurs in numerous places in Saint Paul's letters, including the following passages:

"But *thanks be to God,* that you who were once slaves of sin have become obedient from the heart to the standard of teaching to which you were committed, and, having been set free from sin, have become slaves of righteousness."   — Romans 6:17-18

"Wretched man that I am! Who will deliver me from this body of death? *Thanks be to God* through Jesus Christ our Lord!"   — Romans 7:24-25

"The sting of death is sin, and the power of sin is the law. But *thanks be to God,* who gives us the victory through our Lord Jesus Christ."
— 1 Corinthians 15:56-57

"But *thanks be to God,* who in Christ always leads us in triumph, and through us spreads the fragrance of the knowledge of him everywhere."
— 2 Corinthians 2:14

"*Thanks be to God* for his inexpressible gift!"   — 2 Corinthians 9:15

(emphasis added)

If the Reading is from the Old Testament, we can see how Jesus has responded to it in the Gospel to follow. If the Reading is from the Acts of the Apostles, we can marvel at the power of God's Spirit at work in the early Church as we witness the apostles' transformation, from men who fled at the arrest of Jesus to men willing to undergo their own passion and death for the sake of Christ.

Our response is a response to God's love for us. In our preparation we found, like Saint Paul, that we are as good as dead without God's help. As we listen to the proclamation of God's Word, we joyfully hear that a savior has come — and this indeed is a reason to give thanks to God!

OPPORTUNITY FOR SPIRITUAL GROWTH

- Pay special attention to the First Reading in anticipation of the Gospel.

- See what led the Church to choose this Reading as a complement to the Gospel.

- How does it help explain why the Jewish followers of Jesus saw our Lord as the fulfillment of everything that had been written in the Law and by the prophets?

8

How to Respond to the Responsorial Psalm

CONTENTS OF THIS CHAPTER

- What Are Psalms?
- Reference to Christ?
- The Prayer of Jesus
- The Psalm Response
- Our Response

WHAT ARE PSALMS?

The Book of Psalms is found in the Bible. It is a collection of inspired poems, hymns, and prayers. Traditionally, the Psalms were attributed to King David, but even within the book itself various Psalms are attributed to other authors (i.e., Psalms 44-48, 84-85, and 87-88 are attributed to the "sons of Korah"; Psalms 73-83 are attributed to Asaph). The name of the book is drawn from its Greek name, *psalmos,* which is a translation of the Hebrew word *mizmor,* meaning "a song accompanied by music."

The Psalms were used in the time of Jesus in both the worship services of the temple and the synagogues. Jesus quotes from the Book of Psalms more than from any other book of Scripture. The early Christian Church that, in its beginnings, was part of the Jewish faith, continued to pray the Psalms and found in them a new meaning that only became apparent after the life, death, and Resurrection of Jesus.

The practice of singing a response to the Psalm dates back to the early Church, as can be seen in the quote at the beginning of this chapter from the *Apostolic Constitutions* at the turn of the fourth century A.D.

REFERENCE TO CHRIST?

The disciples instructed by Jesus Himself saw in the Psalms prophecies that were fulfilled by Jesus. In Luke 24:44-45, quoted

" 'These are my words which I spoke to you, while I was still with you, that everything written about me in the law of Moses and the prophets and the psalms must be fulfilled.' Then he opened their minds to understand the scriptures...."

— Luke 24:44-45

in the box above, Jesus told His disciples that the Psalms referred to Him.

The early Church went a step further and regarded the Psalms as revealing the very inner life of Jesus. Father Alexander Schmemann, in his great work *The Eucharist*, wrote about the significance of Christ in the Psalms:

> These are *his* words, *his* prayer: "the Lord Jesus Christ speaks in them" (Augustine). And because they are his words, they are also the prayer and words of his body, the Church. "In this book speak, pray and weep only Jesus Christ and his Church," writes Augustine.

David, inspired by the Holy Spirit, had written words that would only be fully understood when Christ would walk the earth. So when we hear Jesus cry from the cross, "My God, my God, why hast thou forsaken me?" in the Gospels of Matthew and Mark, we are led to Psalm 22, where we read:

> *My God, my God, why hast thou forsaken me?*
> *Why art thou so far from helping me, from the words of*
> *   my groaning?*
> *O my God, I cry by day, but thou dost not answer;*
> *And by night, but find no rest.*
>
> *Yet thou art holy,*
> *Enthroned on the praises of Israel.*

In thee our fathers trusted;
they trusted, and thou didst deliver them.
To thee they cried, and were saved;
in thee they trusted, and were not disappointed.

But I am a worm, and no man;
Scorned by men, and despised by the people.
All who see me mock at me,
They make mouths at me, they wag their heads;
"He committed his cause to the Lord; let him deliver him,
let him rescue him, for he delights in him!"

— Psalm 22:1-8

The prayer continues:

They have pierced my hands and feet —
I can count all my bones —
They stare and gloat over me;
They divide my garments among them,
And for my raiment they cast lots.

— Psalm 22:16-18

Compare this to the account of Jesus' crucifixion in the Gospel of Matthew:

And when they had crucified him, they divided his garments among them by casting lots; then they sat down and kept watch over him there.... And those who passed by derided him, wagging their heads and saying, "You who would destroy the temple and build it in three days, save yourself! If you are the Son of God, come down from that cross." So also the chief priests, with the scribes and elders, mocked him, saying, "He saved others; he cannot save himself. He is the King of Israel; let him come down now from the cross, and we will believe in him. He trusts in God; let God deliver him now,

if he desires him; for he said, 'I am the Son of God.' " And the
robbers who were crucified with him also reviled him in the
same way.... And about the ninth hour Jesus cried with a loud
voice, "Eli, Eli, la'ma sabach-tha'ni?" that is, "My God, my
God, why hast thou forsaken me?"

— Matthew 27:35-36, 39-44, 46

Once we notice the similarity of what Jesus experienced during the crucifixion and the prayer of Psalm 22, the first line of which Jesus is recorded crying out from the cross, we can see how the early followers of Christ made the connection between the Psalms as the prayers of Jesus. Knowing that Jesus is praying Psalm 22 also gives us a different insight on what Jesus' cry from the cross really means.

On the surface it might seem that Jesus was giving in to despair, but when one reads the end of Psalm 22, we find the prayer is anything but a prayer of defeat:

I will tell of thy name to my brethren;
In the midst of the congregation
  I will praise thee:
You who fear the Lord, praise him!
  All you sons of Jacob, glorify him,
  And stand in awe of him, all you sons of Israel!
For he has not despised or abhorred the affliction of the afflicted;
And he has not hid his face from him,
But has heard, when he cried to him.

— Psalm 22:22-24

This example should help you understand how the early Christians accepted the Psalms as the prayer of Jesus Himself.

THE PRAYER OF JESUS

Christians, as Saint Paul points out, are "in Christ" and members of His Mystical Body — the Church. So from early on, the practice of the Body of Christ on earth — i.e., the Church, gathered — was to pray the Psalms daily. When we pray a Psalm we do so mindful that we belong to Christ, that His prayer is our prayer. We join our life's concerns to those who gather with us, and together we offer them to God the Father, who looks upon us and sees His Son.

The Church prays the Book of Psalms throughout the day, around the world. At every hour of each day there are Christians gathered someplace who pray from the Book of Psalms, the prayer of Jesus. The official name of this prayer of the Church is the Liturgy of the Hours, literally the "work of the moment." There are set prayers that are prayed at different times of the day, throughout the day. Anyone can join in this prayer. Some churches and most Catholic monastic communities gather at preset times throughout the day. If you are interested in learning more about praying the Liturgy of the Hours, you can purchase a prayer book in a Catholic bookstore or find several Internet sites that post the prayers (just do a search for "Liturgy of the Hours").

OPPORTUNITY FOR SPIRITUAL GROWTH

As you pray or sing the Responsorial Psalm at Mass, try to imagine Jesus praying the Psalm. Join your praying of it to His.

THE PSALM RESPONSE

The Psalm prayed during the Mass is called the Responsorial Psalm because it responds to the First Reading. This connection should help us to continue our meditation on what God is telling us through His Word. Often a cantor will sing this Psalm (after all, remember that Psalms are "songs to be accompanied by music"), and we will respond with a refrain taken from one line of the Psalm that often pinpoints the connection with the First Reading.

Singing helps us to internalize the message of the Scripture and also is an excellent way to commit large portions of the Bible to memory. Knowing the Scriptures by heart will enable us to pray the Word of God when our lives meet the cross, in perfect imitation of Jesus.

CATHOLIC PRACTICES

 Remember in the last chapter that we showed the connection between the First Reading and the Gospel for the First Sunday of Lent, Cycle A. The First Reading is the account of Adam and Eve succumbing to sin in the Garden of Eden. The Gospel for that Sunday is the account of Jesus being tempted by Satan in the desert. **What is the Responsorial Psalm?**

Psalm 51, a penitential Psalm that declares our sinfulness and need of God's mercy. How do we respond? "Be Merciful, O Lord, for we have sinned."

We acknowledge that we too, like Adam and Eve, have sinned and require the mercy of God.

OUR RESPONSE

Mindful that the Psalm is chosen especially to draw out the meaning of the First Reading and is also the prayer of Jesus and His Body, the Church, we have a lot to reflect upon as we listen to the Psalm chanted and reply with the response of the day.

It is good to listen to the Word of God mindful that our baptism has made us a part of Christ. It is no longer Jesus and me; it is only Jesus who now lives within me. We pray the Psalm through Him, with Him, and in Him. We are totally His.

9

How to Listen to the Second Reading

CONTENTS OF THIS CHAPTER

- Where Is the Second Reading Taken From?
- Continuous Reading
- Letters Written to Churches and the Church
- Our Response

WHERE IS THE SECOND READING TAKEN FROM?

This Reading, like the First Reading and Psalm we have just heard, is taken from the Holy Bible. This Reading is proclaimed from the Lectionary (remember that the Lectionary is a collection of selections taken from the Bible and arranged for use in the Mass). As in the First Reading, there are slight modifications so it makes sense when we hear the selection proclaimed.

The Second Reading, unlike the first, is always from the New Testament. Remember that "testament" is another word for "covenant." The Readings we call the New Testament deal with the coming of Jesus and the establishment of God's New Covenant with humanity through Jesus, God's Son.

The first part of the New Testament is made up of four books called Gospels (a word that means "good news"). The Gospels tell the stories of Jesus' coming, ministry among the Jewish people, His passion, death, and Resurrection.

The second part of the New Testament is made up of the Acts of the Apostles, the Letters of Saint Paul to various churches, the Letter to the Hebrews, the Letters of Saint Peter, the Letters of Saint John, the Letter of Saint James, and the Book of Revelation (sometimes called the Apocalypse).

We consider these Readings to be the Word of God. Mindful that we are in God's Presence, we listen with expectation. What will God say to us?

CONTINUOUS READING

The Second Reading is usually from the same Letter or from the Book of Revelation for several Sundays in a row. Unlike the First Reading and Responsorial Psalm, it is not in concert with the Gospel Reading each Sunday, but rather is a continuation of the previous Sunday's Reading.

Knowing that the Second Reading is a continuous reading should motivate us to pick up our Bible and read and study at home the Letter (or Book of Revelation) that is currently being

---

CATHOLIC PRACTICES

Notice that on these three Sundays, for example, we hear a continuous Reading from Saint Paul's First Letter to the Corinthians, verse for verse:

On the Fourth Sunday in Ordinary Time, Year A

The Second Reading is from Saint Paul's First Letter to the Corinthians, Chapter 1, Verses 26-31.

On the Fifth Sunday in Ordinary Time, Year A

The Second Reading is from Saint Paul's First Letter to the Corinthians, Chapter 2, Verses 1-5.

On the Sixth Sunday in Ordinary Time, Year A

The Second Reading is from Saint Paul's First Letter to the Corinthians, Chapter 2, Verses 6-10.

But then the Church chooses to skip ahead to the middle of the next chapter so we can experience as much of the Letters over a three-year period as possible.

On the Seventh Sunday in Ordinary Time, Year A

The Second Reading is from Saint Paul's First Letter to the Corinthians, Chapter 3, Verses 16-23.

---

read in the liturgical cycle. During the weeks cited in the boxed example on Page 111, it would be a good time for us to read Saint Paul's First Letter to the Corinthians at home, and to study its meaning both for the Church at Corinth (the people Paul originally wrote the Letter to in the first century A.D.), and for us today.

LETTERS WRITTEN TO CHURCHES AND THE CHURCH

The Second Reading is always taken from Letters originally written to different local churches in the lands surrounding the Mediterranean Sea (even the Book of Revelation, which technically isn't a Letter itself, contains letters to seven churches). As such, these Letters were addressed to particular people and were answering questions that we can only glean from the answers.

The early Church held these Letters and the Book of Revelation to be sacred because of their authors and the message they contained. As we sit, attentively listening to the proclamation of these Readings, we may find our own questions answered by them.

OPPORTUNITY FOR SPIRITUAL GROWTH

As you listen to the Second Reading, try to discern what was going on in the church the apostle is addressing. How does it relate to your parish? How might it relate to your life?

OUR RESPONSE

In 2004, the Congregation for Divine Worship and the Discipline of the Sacraments, the Vatican congregation that oversees how the Mass is celebrated throughout the world, released a document called "The Year of the Eucharist: Suggestions and Proposals," in preparation for the Year of the Eucharist called by Pope John Paul II for October 2004-October 2005. Within that document were the following words about how we should respond to the Liturgy of the Word:

Attentiveness to the word spoken is at the beginning of the spiritual life. To believe in Christ is to listen to his word and put it into practice. It is docility to the voice of the Holy Spirit, the interior Master who guides us to the whole truth — not only to the truth to be known, but also to the truth to be lived out.

In order truly to listen to the Lord in the Liturgy of the Word, we need to learn how to "listen with the heart." This capacity to "listen with the heart" requires that we set aside specific moments of the day, and not just our leftover scraps of time, to dedicate ourselves to reading Sacred Scripture. And so that the message heard in the Eucharistic Celebration not be lost the moment we leave the church doors, it is convenient to find ways to prolong the hearing of God's word, which he speaks to us in a thousand different ways through the circumstances of daily life, throughout the day.

What we hear proclaimed in all of the Readings is the Word of the Lord, and when we say "Thanks be to God" we should be mindful that our thankfulness for the gift received is truly spoken by the way we allow it to shape our lives.

10

How to Listen to the Gospel

CONTENTS OF THIS CHAPTER

- The Gospel Acclamation — Alleluia
- When the Alleluia Is Replaced
- The Good News
- Preparation of the Deacon or Priest to Proclaim the Gospel
- Guarding Our Minds, Lips, and Hearts
- The Proclamation of the Gospel
- Our Response

THE GOSPEL ACCLAMATION — ALLELUIA

After the Second Reading, we reach the high point of the Liturgy of the Word, for we are about to hear the Gospel proclaimed. This occurs with great solemnity, beginning with the singing of the Alleluia verse. This can be done a number of ways, but it should always awaken within us the thought that we are about to hear something very special.

As we stand, the priest or deacon moves toward the altar to take the Book of the Gospels, an ornate book that contains the Gospel Readings for each Sunday (again these are selections taken from the Holy Bible). Father Alexander Schmemann said in his book *The Eucharist*:

> For the Church, the gospel book is a verbal icon of Christ's manifestation to and presence among us. Above all, it is an icon of his resurrection.... It is the image of the appearance of the risen Lord in fulfillment of his promise: "where two or three are gathered in my name, there am I in the midst of them" (Mt 18:20).

The minister who will read the Gospel is joined by two candle bearers called "acolytes" (a Greek word that means "attendants"), and an another acolyte who bears incense (in Masses during which incense is being used).

As we sing the Alleluia, the Gospel is held aloft and carried in procession to the pulpit. This is done with great solemnity, for the words we are about to hear are the words of Jesus Christ, the Word of God.

Although all the Readings we hear proclaimed at Mass are the Word of God, the Gospel is pre-eminent because it is the Word of God made manifest in the telling of Jesus' life, death, and Resurrection. This is why these Readings are in a special, ornate book, and why this book is taken from the altar to the pulpit in great procession.

— WHAT DOES IT MEAN? —

"Alleluia" is the Greek form of the Hebrew word "*Hallelu Yah*," which means "Praise the Lord!" or more literally "Praise *Yahweh*!" "*Yahweh*" was the sacred name of God never pronounced by anyone except the High Priest, and then only once a year. So whenever the name of God appeared in the Scriptures, the reader would say "*Adonai*" instead. "*Adonai*" is a Hebrew word that means "Lord."

As you watch the Book of the Gospels being held aloft, think about all of those who awaited the coming of God's Messiah. Open your own heart to the many needs found there and ask the Holy Spirit to make you attentive so that this time of visitation will not idly pass you by. Everything happening in the church at this moment is trying to alert us to this moment when we shall hear proclaimed the good news that God has become one of us and walked in our midst.

WHEN THE ALLELUIA IS REPLACED

During the Lenten Season the Alleluia is not sung or said. But unlike the Gloria, which is omitted altogether during Advent and Lent, the Alleluia is replaced with another verse that gives praise to the Lord.

The Book of the Gospels is still carried in solemn procession during the season of Lent, but the absence of the Alleluia alerts us to a time of meditation on our human condition, our need for salvation, and the anticipation of Easter, when the Alleluia will return with great solemnity.

THE GOOD NEWS

"Gospel" literally means "good news." What is this good news that we are about to hear? It is the message of Jesus Christ, our Lord and Savior.

I am reminded of a priest who once went into the pulpit with the daily newspaper. He opened it and began reading various headlines: man murdered, accident kills family of five, governor loses battle with cancer ... on and on it went — literally "bad news," but the news that makes up our daily lives as human beings. So what is the "good news"?

When Jesus was asked by the disciples of John the Baptist who He was, His reply was for them to return to John and tell him that "the blind receive their sight and the lame walk, lepers are cleansed and the deaf hear, and the dead are raised up, and the poor have good news preached to them. And blessed is he who takes no offense at me" (Matthew 11:5-6). This is the effect of the "good news" that Jesus said the poor have preached to them. It is an answer to all the bad news that we encounter in our daily lives.

Jesus told His disciples that God's original plan for creation is so much better than what we humans often choose. If we believe God loves us and empowers us to do His will, no matter what obstacles lie in the way, if we follow the path that Jesus has walked before us, we accept the "good news." Then we are "blessed," for we have not "taken offense" in Jesus.

PREPARATION OF THE DEACON OR PRIEST TO PROCLAIM THE GOSPEL

Before the priest takes the Book of the Gospels and begins the procession toward the pulpit, he says a prayer asking God to be in his heart and on his lips, that he may worthily proclaim the Gospel. If a deacon is reading the Gospel, he will receive a blessing from the priest or bishop, who will say a similar prayer over the deacon.

The priest or deacon greets the congregation by once again asking that the Lord be with them. The people respond by asking that the same be the case with the minister proclaiming the Gospel.

The minister announces which Gospel today's selection is from, to which the people respond, "Glory to you, O Lord!" This should be a joyful response, one said with gratitude for all God has done for us in sending His Son to save us.

If incense is used, he then incenses the Book of the Gospels. Incense is a unique way of showing that something is sacred and worthy of being treated in a special manner (see Page 161 for more about incense). It reminds us that the words contained within this book are unlike any other.

The minister at this point makes the sign of the cross over the Gospel Reading and then on his forehead, lips, and heart. All of those in attendance also trace the sign of the cross on their foreheads, lips, and hearts.

GUARDING OUR MINDS, LIPS, AND HEARTS

Listening to the "good news" is not easy when so many other messages are vying for our attention. Jesus warned His disciples, using the parable of the sower, that once the Word of God has been sown into the hearts of believers, "then the devil comes and takes away the word from their hearts, that they may not believe and be saved" (Luke 8:12).

HOW TO MAKE THE SIGN OF THE CROSS ON YOUR FOREHEAD, LIPS, AND HEART BEFORE LISTENING TO THE GOSPEL

Using your thumb, trace the sign of the cross first on your forehead, then your lips, and finally over your heart as you say:

"May the Lord purify my understanding, my speech, and my heart, so that I may receive the words of the Gospel."

Allowing the Gospel to sink into our lives not only requires letting go of the preconceived notions that dominate our thoughts, our words, and our emotions, but also calls for an act of faith. Jesus tells us evil forces do not wish for us to give our assent. For this reason it is customary to make the sign of the cross (a way of thwarting evil) over our foreheads, over our lips, and over our hearts in preparation to truly hear the Gospel.

The meaning of this ritual according to the great historian Father Jungmann, in his work *Mass of the Roman Rite*, is:

> For the word which Christ brought and which is set down in this book we are willing to stand up with a mind that is open; we are ready to confess it with our mouth; and above all we are determined to safeguard it faithfully in our hearts.

In the Eastern Church, a deacon will proclaim, "wisdom be attentive!" Making the sign of the cross over our foreheads, lips, and hearts should have the same effect on us. It should make us attentive to what we are about to hear — the saving message of the Gospel.

THE PROCLAMATION OF THE GOSPEL

Everything that comes before this point in the Mass is preparation for us to listen to Jesus speaking to us in the Gospel. The special nature of this Reading is emphasized by our standing to hear it, the candles and incense, the ornate style of the book that contains the Readings, the ordained minister who proclaims it, the special prayer and blessing he says or receives in order to proclaim it, the joyful response we give upon hearing that we are about to hear the Gospel giving glory to God, and the final act of tracing the sign of the cross over the forehead, lips, and heart in order to repel the evil one from snatching the fruit of this message.

As the *General Instruction for the Roman Missal* says, we stand to "acknowledge and confess Christ present and speaking" to us.

The word "Gospel" appears throughout the New Testament referring to the proclamation of the Lord's victory over sin, death, and all evil. The following are a few examples:

"And truly, I say to you, wherever the *gospel* is preached in the whole world, what she has done will be told in memory of her."

— Mark 14:9

"And this *gospel* of the kingdom will be preached throughout the whole world, as a testimony to all nations; and then the end will come."

— Matthew 24:14

"Then I saw another angel flying in midheaven, with an eternal *gospel* to proclaim to those who dwell on earth, to every nation and tribe and tongue and people...."

— Revelation 14:6

(emphasis added)

Listen to the Gospel to see how Jesus has revealed God perfectly to us. Does the Gospel that I hear proclaimed match my understanding of God?

Philip the Apostle once said to Jesus, "Lord, show us the Father, and we shall be satisfied." To which Jesus replied, "Have I been with you so long, and yet you do not know me, Philip? He who has seen me has seen the Father ..." (John 14:8-9).

In listening to the Gospel we come to "see" Jesus and learn what God is like and what God wishes of us.

OUR RESPONSE

At the end of the Gospel proclamation, the minister kisses the Book of the Gospels, then holds it aloft as he announces to us that what we have heard is the "Gospel of the Lord." We answer by giving praise to our Lord Jesus Christ — "Praise to you, Lord Jesus Christ" — for all He has done for us, not only in revealing God to us, but in opening the way of salvation to us.

OPPORTUNITY FOR SPIRITUAL GROWTH

Reflect on what the Gospel reveals to you today about the "good news." Ask our Lord to make you a better disciple.

11

How to Hear a Great Homily — *Every Time* You Attend Mass

CONTENTS OF THIS CHAPTER

- What Is a Homily?
- Praying for the Preacher
- Listening to a Homily
- Meditation — "... [Jesus] interpreted to them in all the scriptures ..."

WHAT IS A HOMILY?

A homily is an interpretation of the Readings we have just heard proclaimed and an application of what they mean to us today. Jesus constantly explained the Scriptures to His disciples, and they in turn continued to do so to those to whom they preached after Jesus' Ascension.

In the Gospel passage we are using in this book as a meditation on the Mass (Luke 24:27), Jesus explains the Scriptures to the disciples on the road to Emmaus. He does so in response to what they are discussing when He joins them. Our Lord puts the events of their lives into the context of what has been revealed in Scripture. Their response is recorded later when they tell the apostles that their "hearts burned" as the Lord opened the Scriptures to them.

In the first homily recorded in Scripture, Peter preaches to the crowds on the day of Pentecost and first responds to their contention that the disciples are drunk. He declares that they are not drunk, but explains what has happened by referring to Scripture. He gives witness to the power of God working in their midst.

Ideally, this is what every homily does. It brings the Scriptures into the present moment. A great homily will make our "hearts burn" for Christ by enlightening us to the great need we have to be in communion with Him.

When our Lord finished opening the Scriptures to the disciples on the road to Emmaus, He began to separate Himself from them.

They begged Him to stay with them. A great homily will create the same sentiment within us: We will beg the Lord to stay with us!

At the end of Peter's preaching, the people didn't walk away, satiated; rather, they asked Peter, "What must we do?"

WHAT IS IT?

A great homily is not one that answers all of our questions or is necessarily entertaining. Rather, a great homily is one that troubles us, or one that challenges us, or one that leaves us dissatisfied.

A great homily will whet our appetite for Jesus and our reception of Him in the Eucharist.

PRAYING FOR THE PREACHER

The preacher has an awesome task. It is easy to see why the Church is so guarded in whom it allows to preach. We should always silently offer a prayer for the deacon, priest, or bishop who is preaching, asking God to send His Holy Spirit upon him so that through the homily, we will be moved to a deeper relationship with God.

Of course, a benefit that we will receive when we pray for the preacher is that we will listen with the expectation that God will answer our prayer and inspire the preacher to deliver a great homily.

If we prejudge the homilist and dismiss his ability because of the way we have perceived his abilities in the past, we ourselves will suffer.

I had a friend who did this on a regular basis. Once, when he saw who was preaching, he leaned over to me at Mass and whispered in my ear, "This guy has never preached a decent homily in his entire life." You can be assured that my friend did not hear a great homily that day. In fact, he didn't really hear any homily at all — he pulled out a book he had brought with him and read it while the priest preached a "great" homily to the rest of us.

LISTENING TO A HOMILY

Listening to a homily is very much like listening to the Scriptures. It requires our whole attention. If we really believe that God is going to speak to us, we will hang on every word the homilist speaks, expecting to receive a unique message that God intends for us.

In the early Church, certain holy men and women retired to the desert to devote themselves entirely to acts of asceticism and prayer. People, believing those souls to be close to God, would often trek out to the desert specifically to receive a "word" from the desert father or mother, and sometimes that is all they would receive. Listen to every homily at Mass expecting that God will speak a "word" to you. No matter how poor the presentation, or how long or short it is, if we expect to hear a "word" from God, we will — and we will hear a great homily at every Mass!

In the Masses I have attended while writing this book, I have put this into practice. I have heard several different bishops preach, at least seven different priests, and one deacon. There have been several times when it didn't seem like God would speak a "word" to me through a particular preacher, but then it would happen: The preacher would say something simple but timely that spoke directly to me.

I wrote an article some years ago about people who complain that they "are not being fed" by poor preaching in the Catholic Church. In it I spoke of the Israelites in the desert who complained against Moses that they were sick of the manna that God was providing them. Our attitude has a lot to do with whether we are "being fed" at Mass. If we first ask God to speak a "word" to us, God will! But we should also be mindful that the homily is not the end; it will ideally make us hungry for more, and the "more" is God.

THE FAITH OF THE EARLY CHURCH

The following story illustrates the principle of seekers going out in the desert in hopes of having a "word" given to them by a desert father (in this case Saint Antony). The story also illustrates the need to pray for receptivity to the "word" once it is given:

"Certain brethren once came to Saint Antony and besought him to speak to them some word through which they might attain unto the perfection of salvation. He, however, said to them, 'Ye have heard the Scriptures. The words which have come from the lips of Christ for your learning are sufficient for you.' When they still pressed him, begging that he would deign to speak some word to them, he said, 'It is taught in the gospel that if a man smite you on the one cheek you are to turn to him the other also.' They then confessed that they were not able to do this. Saint Antony answered, 'Is this too hard for you? Are you willing to let such a man strike you on the same cheek twice?' They said, 'We are not willing,' hoping to be told of some easier thing. But he said to them, 'If this, too, is beyond you, at least do not render evil for evil.' Again they answered him as they had done before. Then Saint Antony turned to his disciple who stood by, and said, 'Prepare some food and give it to these men, for they are weak.' But to the brethren who had inquired of him, he said, 'If you cannot do one thing and will not do another, why do you come seeking a word of exhortation from me? To me it seems that what you need most is to pray. By prayer perhaps you may be healed of your infirmity.' "

— *The Way of the Fathers*,
Book IV, Chapter VI

MEDITATION

And beginning with Moses and all the prophets, he interpreted to them in all the scriptures the things concerning himself.

— Luke 24:27

"... [Jesus] interpreted to them in all the scriptures ..."

The disciples on the road to Emmaus did not recognize our Lord as He opened and interpreted the Scriptures to them — to them He was still a stranger. Yet later, they would reflect that their hearts burned as He spoke.

We may not recognize our Lord in those who preach to us at first, but if our hearts are open to not only receiving His Word but allowing it to take root in our lives, we, too, may find our hearts will "burn" with a fire that fills us with God's love.

WHERE IS IT IN SCRIPTURE?

God speaks a "word" and it comes into existence:

"And God said, 'Let there be light'; and there was light."

— Genesis 1:3

God's "word" is efficacious:

"For as the rain and the snow come down from heaven, and return not thither but water the earth, making it bring forth and sprout, giving seed to the sower and bread to the eater, so shall my word be that goes forth from my mouth; it shall not return to me empty, but it shall accomplish that which I purpose, and prosper in the thing for which I sent it."

— Isaiah 55:10-11

The Scriptures are the Word of God. They have an effect. When God created the world, He did so by speaking a "word."

In the same way, when we have the Word of God proclaimed to us, the Word will take root in our lives — if we are fertile soil. We will see, like the disciples who walked with our Lord on the road to Emmaus, that our lives are not meaningless — that the events that happen to us today take on new meaning when the light of the Word of God shines on them.

Good preaching, as I have said earlier, does not answer all our questions. It does not entertain us, either; sometimes it may even bore us as we listen. We may find that we don't understand it. But later, at a moment of God's own choosing, we will be surprised when suddenly something that was said makes perfect sense and fits the need of the present moment.

Our Lord alerted His disciples to be watchful, for we know neither the day nor the hour when He will come again. Every Mass should be spent in complete expectation of the Lord's coming. As we listen to His words, in our hearts we repeat, "Come, Lord!" As the preacher speaks, we silently pray, "Come, Lord!" He will.

12

Time Out! Where Are *They* Going and Who Are They?

CONTENTS OF THIS CHAPTER

- Dismissal of Catechumens
- Responding to the Word
- Praying for the Catechumens and Candidates
- Where Are They Going?
- Meditation — " 'Stay with us ...' "

DISMISSAL OF CATECHUMENS

After the homily, catechumens and candidates for full communion are dismissed. If you are a lifelong Catholic and were baptized as an infant, you may be confused by this.

I remember a Catholic who was horrified when she witnessed the dismissal of catechumens for the first time. The catechumens, an entire family of African-Americans, were dismissed at the appropriate time. The Catholic, who had never seen anyone have to leave a Mass during her lifetime, interpreted this as an act of racism. "It's terrible what they are making those poor people do," she said.

Call it a case of poor catechizing, but of course this was not an example of the Church trying to prevent anyone from joining. Rather, what my Catholic friend was witnessing was the restoration of an ancient practice called the Catechumenate, a process of formation in the Gospel and the Christian faith leading to full initiation into the Church.

If you are an older Catholic, you may recall that the Liturgy of the Word was always referred to as the Mass of the Catechumens at a time when there were no "catechumens." After the Second Vatican Council, the Church sought to restore many of the practices of the early Church. The Catechumenate is one of those practices that has been restored.

THE FAITH OF THE EARLY CHURCH

"Let us all pray unto God for the catechumens, that He who is good, He who is the lover of mankind, will mercifully hear their prayers and their supplications, and so accept their petitions to assist them and give them the desires of their hearts which are for their advantage, and reveal to them the Gospel of His Christ...."

— *Apostolic Constitutions*, A.D. 400

Not everyone who leaves during the dismissal is technically a "catechumen." A catechumen is someone who has not yet been baptized a Christian; yet there are those who have been baptized Christians, but are not Catholics. If such a person expresses interest in joining the Catholic Church, he, too, enters a process of formation similar to the Catechumenate but is known as a "candidate for full communion," because he has been baptized already. Candidates for full communion are confirmed and receive their First Holy Communion at the end of the process. Catechumens will be baptized, confirmed, and receive the Eucharist at the end of their formation.

Those who have gone through the experience of leaving each week, whether as catechumens or candidates for full communion, find the process gives them time to reflect upon the great gift the Catholic faith is, something that those of us who are cradle Catholics may not appreciate.

RESPONDING TO THE WORD

We have mentioned that when we hear the Word of God proclaimed and preached, it requires a response from us. The catechumens and candidates for full communion are symbols to us of the type of response required of all of us. They journey in faith trying to learn more about Christ and His Church in order to fully embrace the Catholic faith. Those of us who have already made this commitment need to recall how well we are living out our baptism and continuing to grow in our relationship with Christ.

The sacrifices that the catechumens and candidates make to become Catholics are a testament to what a great gift the faith is. Do you and I recognize this, or have we grown lukewarm in our response to God's gracious gift?

PRAYING FOR THE CATECHUMENS AND CANDIDATES

When the catechumens and candidates for full communion are called forth for the dismissal, you and I should ask the Lord to bless them on their journey of faith. If we do not know any of the catechumens or candidates, we should try to introduce ourselves to them, making them feel welcome and assuring them that we are praying for them.

What kind of prayers should we pray for those who wish to join us in the Catholic Church?

You can answer this question for yourself by reflecting on what type of prayers you say on a regular basis. If you pray the Rosary, say a decade for those preparing for baptism in your parish. If you pray the Liturgy of the Hours, add a special intention during the intercessions at Morning and Evening Prayer for them.

If you are really curious about what the catechumens and candidates are going through, contact the person in charge of the program in your parish and ask them. You may be able to serve on a Catechumenate team as a sponsor or in another position.

WHERE ARE THEY GOING?

A Catechumenate leader holds the Book of the Gospels aloft as he or she leads the catechumens and candidates for full communion out of the Church and into a space where they will spend the rest of the Mass reflecting on and sharing the meaning of the Scriptures. Even though we remain as they leave, we should imitate what they will do by meditating on all that we have heard, too. Like the Blessed Virgin Mary who heard the Word of God and "wondered" what it could mean, we, too, should reflect.

MEDITATION

So they drew near to the village to which they were going. [Jesus] appeared to be going further, but they constrained him, saying, "Stay with us, for it is toward evening and the day is now far spent." So he went in to stay with them.

— Luke 24:28-29

" 'Stay with us …' "

When the disciples who accompanied the stranger on the road to Emmaus had heard Him open the Scriptures and their meaning to them, they suddenly reached their destination. At that point the Gospel tells us that Jesus was ready to leave them to continue His journey.

The disciples were so overwhelmed with His teaching that they asked Him to stay with them.

If you have opened your heart and all of your thoughts and worries to our Lord in this Mass, you will find yourself in the same situation. As you watch those who leave the church building now because they have not yet fully accepted the Catholic faith, reflect that you remain behind because you have through your baptism asked the Lord to stay with you. The Lord has revealed Himself in His Word today, and now He awaits your response, again.

Do you implore Him to "stay" with you?

I have mentioned earlier in this book an ancient Christian prayer: *Maranatha*, "Come, Lord." As the catechumens and candidates for full communion leave the church, ask the Lord to come to them, and ask Him to come to you, too.

"Stay with us, Lord." May this always be our response to the Readings we hear proclaimed at every Mass.

13

How to Pray the Creed

CONTENTS OF THIS CHAPTER

- The Response of the Faithful
- I Believe ...
- ... In One God
- ... In Jesus Christ
- ... In the Holy Spirit and the Catholic Church
- ... In the Resurrection of the Body and Life Everlasting
- Renewal of Baptismal Promises
- Meditation — "He appeared to be going further ..."

THE RESPONSE OF THE FAITHFUL

Earlier we mentioned that at the Covenant of Mount Sinai, Moses read the Covenant of the Law and when he finished, the people proclaimed, "All that the Lord has said we will do." In the Mass of the New Covenant, we, too, are faced with a decision. We have heard the Word of God proclaimed and preached. Now, how will we respond?

The Church gives us a prayer to recite as our response. It is a prayer composed at the Council of Nicea in A.D. 325 in response to those who were teaching as Christianity doctrines that the bishops gathered at the council deemed not to be truly Christian. The bishops composed a summary of what Christians truly believe: a creed (a word that comes from the first word of a creed in Latin: *Credo* — "I believe").

In the Eastern Catholic and Orthodox churches, the creed was inserted into the Mass soon after the Council of Nicea. In that region the Church had been particularly hard hit by the Arian heresy (more than a third of the bishops of the time were themselves believers in this heresy). So for those believers in the Eastern Church, the creed served as a way to purify the Church of any faulty beliefs that remained after the declarations of the council.

The creed was used in the Western Church in baptismal preparation but not in the Mass until the eleventh century. The creed is an opportunity for the believer to declare that he believes in God as He has been revealed in the Scriptures and through the teaching of the Church. As the *General Instruction of the Roman Missal,* the official guide to the Mass, states, the creed "serves as a way for the people to respond and give assent to the Word of God."

This is our opportunity to respond to God's Word.

First, you may recall that a group of people has just been dismissed from the Mass — the catechumens, who have not been baptized, and the candidates, who have not yet fully embraced the Catholic faith. Those of us who remain have both been baptized and accepted the Catholic Church as the Church that Jesus Christ founded. It is time for us to state that belief publicly.

Second, we, like the people who heard Moses read the Law to them, recite the creed as our way of saying, "All that the Lord has said we will do." By reciting this summation of the Church's belief, we declare ourselves both full members of the Church and faithful disciples of our Lord.

I BELIEVE ...

You may have prayed this prayer for so long that you can say it without reflecting on its meaning. What does it mean to say that you "believe"?

Often today we use the word "believe" in a way that doesn't convey a whole lot of faith. If I say, "I believe the Florida Gators will win the National Championship this year in NCAA football," I'm expressing my opinion. That is not what we are doing when we say that we "believe" in God.

What "believe" means in this instance is that we put all of our trust, indeed our very lives, in God. It might be said that anytime we get on an airplane that someone else is flying, we are saying (without saying it) that we "believe" in the pilot. If we thought that the pilot of the plane was less than trustworthy, we would probably get off the plane.

Think about this as you say the creed at Mass: "I believe in (put all my trust, indeed I'm betting my entire life on) one God...."

The creed celebrates our belief and absolute trust in God.

CATECHISM OF THE CATHOLIC CHURCH

The *Compendium of the Catechism of the Catholic Church* answers the question: "What does it mean to believe in only one God?"

"To believe in the one and only God involves coming to know his greatness and majesty. It involves living in thanksgiving and trusting always in him, even in adversity. It involves knowing the unity and true dignity of all human beings, created in his image. It involves making good use of the things which he has created."

— *Compendium*, No. 43

... IN ONE GOD

There is only one God. Christians hold the belief in one God along with Jews and Muslims. It is important to note that our statement of belief does not say we believe in three Gods. Many good Christians misunderstand the Church's belief in the Trinity (stating belief in one God, but often acting like there are three).

When Philip asked Jesus to show the Father to the apostles, Jesus responded that anyone who had seen Him, had seen the Father. It is important to remember that and to understand that Jesus has revealed God perfectly to us.

... IN JESUS CHRIST

Belief in Jesus is still belief in one God. The Lord became one of us, taking on human flesh and becoming fully human but still fully God as well. This is a mystery and attempts to simplify its teaching are often heretical.

The creed reaches its zenith when we state that for our salvation God became one of us and was made man. Traditionally, in the Western Church, the faithful would genuflect, lowering themselves to honor the supreme mystery of God becoming one of us, at the words "By the Holy Spirit, he was incarnate of the Virgin Mary, and became man." This is still done during the praying of the creed on the solemnity of the Annunciation and at Christmas. Both are feasts of the Church that celebrate the mystery of God becoming one of us, one at His conception, the other at His birth. During the rest of the Church year, we make a solemn bow at these words. This mystery is called the Incarnation, a word that means "taking on human flesh"; in this case, God taking on our human flesh in Jesus Christ.

HOW TO BOW DURING THE CREED

When we pray the creed, we make a profound bow at these words:

"... By the Holy Spirit, he was incarnate of the Virgin Mary, and became man."

At Christmas and the solemnity of the Annunciation of the Lord, we genuflect rather than bow, commemorating the act of God lowering Himself to become man.

There are different types of bows in Catholic liturgical practice.

1. **At the mention of the name of Jesus, there is a slight bow of the head called a simple bow. (This is also done at the mention of any of the three divine persons, the Blessed Virgin Mary, or the saint whose feast is being celebrated on that particular day.)**

2. **A solemn bow involves bending at the waist and touching one's palms to one's knees. This is done when bowing toward the altar, during the creed, and before receiving Holy Communion under either form.**

Because everything depends upon this act of our Lord and makes our salvation possible, the final part of the creed celebrates the grace that we have received from our Lord's death and Resurrection.

... IN THE HOLY SPIRIT AND THE CATHOLIC CHURCH

In the third part of the creed we declare our belief in the Holy Spirit, who animates the Church. The Holy Spirit is described as the "Lord and Giver of Life." God's Spirit is given to us at our baptism.

We say that we believe in "one, holy, catholic and apostolic Church." Our faith is that the Lord has founded a universal Church, built up on the foundation of the apostles (Ephesians 2:20), made up of believers from every part of the world. No one is excluded from our Lord's invitation: The doors have been opened to all who answer the call of Jesus. Saint Paul proclaims, "There is neither Jew nor Greek, there is neither slave nor free, there is neither male nor female; for you are all one in Christ Jesus" (Galatians 3:28).

It is important that we mean what we say when we profess our faith. Any church that calls itself Catholic but closes the door to people who are not of the same ethnic group as the majority is not living up to its name.

There is no such animal as the American Catholic Church or the French Catholic Church or the Italian Catholic Church. The

---

CATECHISM OF THE CATHOLIC CHURCH

"... In death, the separation of the soul from the body, the human body decays and the soul goes to meet God, while awaiting its reunion with its glorified body. God, in his almighty power, will definitively grant incorruptible life to our bodies by reuniting them with our souls, through the power of Jesus' Resurrection." — *CCC*, No. 997

Catholic Church is a universal Church recognizing that Christ has called all people to share in His sacrifice and banquet.

... IN THE RESURRECTION OF THE BODY AND LIFE EVERLASTING

It bears mentioning that we also profess our faith that God will raise our mortal bodies in the same way that Jesus rose from the dead. Our belief in the Assumption of Mary, our Lord's mother and His first disciple, all point to this.

How this will happen is a mystery. Obviously, some people suffer horrible deaths and their bodies are destroyed in the process. Other bodies are cremated. Yet the belief of the Church has always been that at the Last Judgment, God will raise the living and the dead. Some of the Church Fathers reflecting on this mystery have said that everybody will be perfect in heaven. Saint Augustine held that everybody would be thirty-three, the age of our Lord at His Resurrection (regardless of when the person had died — even if they died before they reached their thirty-third birthday). The resurrected would be in perfect conformity to Christ, whereas before, he or she was conformed to Adam.

The point is that for the Christian, the body is important. It is not something to be abused or mistreated. We will spend all of

---

CATECHISM OF THE CATHOLIC CHURCH

"Each man receives his eternal retribution in his immortal soul at the very moment of his death, in a particular judgment that refers his life to Christ: either entrance into the blessedness of heaven — through a purification or immediately, — or immediate and everlasting damnation."

The *Catechism* adds to this a quote from Saint John of the Cross:

"At the evening of life, we shall be judged on our love." — *CCC*, No. 1022

---

eternity with the body God has given us. As Saint Paul says, "Your body is a temple of the Holy Spirit ..." (1 Corinthians 6:19).

Life everlasting is another element of our faith as Christians. Perhaps we do not reflect upon this enough. Everything in our experience points to our life ending when we die. It is faith that gives us sure hope of a continued existence after death. But what shall that life after death be like? The Gospels reflect that we will be judged, and that judgment will grant us ultimately an eternal bliss with God, or eternal damnation.

RENEWAL OF BAPTISMAL PROMISES

At the Easter Vigil and on Easter Sunday, the Renewal of Baptismal Promises takes the place of the creed (see Page 88). Instead of everyone reciting the Profession of Faith, the priest asks a series of questions, to which we respond ("I do"). In the same way a married couple responds when entering into the sacred covenant of marriage, so we in a very literal way renew the covenant with God that we entered into at our baptism.

There are six questions. The first three cover what we promise to turn away from, and the last three affirm what we turn toward. The priest asks us if we reject Satan, his works, and the emptiness of all his lies. Another form of these three questions may begin by asking us if we reject sin, its glamour, and Satan.

The priest then asks us if we believe in tenets of the creed, asking three questions that summarize each aspect of it. After we affirm that we do, in fact, believe, he prays a prayer over the congregation, asking God to keep us faithful to our baptismal vows. The priest then sprinkles us with blessed (holy) water from the baptismal font.

This way of affirming our faith on Easter brings home our ratification of the New Covenant of Jesus Christ. Our "I do's" ring out like the affirmation of the Israelites in the desert, and the priest sprinkling us with baptismal water reminds us of Moses sprinkling the Israelites with the blood of the sacrificed animal. But it is our Lord's sacrifice on the cross that has sealed this New Covenant, and as we are sprinkled with holy water we make the sign of the cross over ourselves, recalling the reason for our hope.

MEDITATION

So they drew near to the village to which they were going. [Jesus] appeared to be going further, but they constrained him, saying, "Stay with us, for it is toward evening and the day is now far spent." So he went in to stay with them.

— Luke 24:28-29

"He appeared to be going further …"

After our Lord had opened the Scriptures to the disciples and they approached the village of Emmaus, Saint Luke tells us that our Lord "appeared to be going further …" (Luke 24:28).

No matter how long we live or how many times we hear the Scriptures proclaimed, we will always find that our Lord at this juncture appears to be "going further" than where we are. This is why the spiritual life is one of constant conversion, constant dying to self in order that we may belong fully to our Lord.

Every event of our life can either be a blessing or a challenge to our faith. The disciples on the road to Emmaus had their faith in Jesus challenged when they watched Him suffer the humiliation of crucifixion and death. There are events in our life when we, too, will encounter both the crucified Lord and the scandal of the cross. If we are open to the proclamation of the Scriptures, we will find that they speak to us, set our hearts on fire, and challenge us to grow ever closer to God.

Then it is up to us, encountering the Lord who seems to always be "going further," to invite Him into the fabric of our lives. We need to put faith in Him, not in our own estimation of the events of our lives. Reciting the creed and renewing our baptismal promises are ways to once again say, "I believe in you, Lord, no matter what may happen."

OPPORTUNITY FOR SPIRITUAL GROWTH

It is easy to recite the creed without really thinking about what you are stating as your belief. Saints have been martyred for these words. We should reflect upon them and try to come to a deeper understanding of them. Reading the *Catechism of the Catholic Church*, the *Compendium of the Catholic Church*, or the *United States Catholic Catechism for Adults* can be a great aid in learning more about the meaning of the different elements of the creed.

14

How to Pray the Prayers of the Faithful

CONTENTS OF THIS CHAPTER

- Acting on Faith
- Lord, Hear Our Prayer
- Universal Prayer
- Meditation — "... they constrained him ..."

ACTING ON FAITH

The Scriptures have been proclaimed. We have declared in our Profession of Faith that we believe in one God who has taken on human flesh in Jesus to save us, and that He has sent the Holy Spirit so that we, as Saint Paul says, might have Christ living within us (Cf. Galatians 2:20).

Now we act as Christ, the mediator between God and man. We allow Christ within us to respond to the promptings of the Holy Spirit to intercede to the Father as we present our needs to Him.

We may not think of ourselves as priests, but this is the teaching of the Church. We are not ordained, but we are called to perform many of the same acts that the ordained priest does in a very public way.

Sometimes the Prayers of the Faithful can be done in a rather rote and unremarkable way. This is a sad commentary, perhaps, on how seriously we take our obligation as Christians to make a difference in the world by offering prayers to God.

Prayer is an act of faith. Do we believe, as Jesus says in the Scriptures, "if you ask anything of the Father, he will give it to you in my name" (John 16:23)? We cannot deny any responsibility for the evils in the world and in our community, if we do not pray. Jesus told His disciples, and that means us, that "if you have faith as a grain of mustard seed, you will say to this mountain, 'Move from here to there,' and it will move; and nothing will be impossible to you" (Matthew 17:20).

How do we view the mountainous obstacles we encounter in life?

In the Book of Exodus 17:11, the Israelites were winning in battle as long as Moses had his arms lifted to God. But when Moses tired and his hands dropped, the Israelites began losing the battle. Others had to stand at Moses' side to hold his hands aloft, so that once again God would bless the Israelites.

So it is, God involves us in the salvation of the world. But this requires our joining our own sacrifices with that of Jesus. God the Father hears our prayers through His Son who lives in us — to whom we are grafted like a gigantic vine (see John 15:1-10).

LORD, HEAR OUR PRAYER

The response to the Prayers of the Faithful usually is "Lord, hear our prayer," although other responses may be used at times. When we address the "Lord," it is God we are summoning.

Another way of phrasing "Lord, hear our prayer" is "God, listen to what we are asking."

We address God out of the belief that He cares about us. Unlike other religions in which God is aloof, Christians believe that God is intensely interested in their lives. The God we believe in acts in the events of our lives, and desires that we be in relationship with Him. We have only to remember our Lord Jesus Christ's example. He has perfectly revealed God to us. Anything we believe about God is revealed perfectly by Jesus because Jesus is God. This is why the Liturgy of the Word is so important. The Scriptures that are read during the Mass remind us again of how Jesus has revealed what God is really like.

People constantly came to Jesus requesting help during His earthly life. When He ascended into heaven they continued to come to His disciples (cf. Acts of the Apostles), who continued to do the same works that Jesus had done, because He was now living in each of them.

Through our baptism, Jesus lives in us. But we must die to ourselves so that His power may operate in our lives. As you hear the Prayers of the Faithful, make them yours by responding with a sense of urgency and faith that the Lord will hear our prayer.

We address these prayers through our Lord Jesus Christ, confident that He will present them to the Father.

UNIVERSAL PRAYER

The Prayers of the Faithful also bring to mind the last part of the creed. We believe in one holy catholic Church. Our membership in the Body of Christ is not a local or national membership, but rather one that extends across the world and, in fact, transcends both time and space (because it also includes those who have gone before us and now live in Christ).

The *General Instruction of the Roman Missal* (the official guidebook of the Mass) says that in the Prayers of the Faithful, we exercise our priestly role in interceding for all of humanity.

Our minds are often filled with images of suffering from around the world. As Catholics we should never forget that it is our duty to intercede endlessly on the behalf of all people.

MEDITATION

[Jesus] appeared to be going further, but they constrained him, saying, "Stay with us, for it is toward evening and the day is now far spent." So he went in to stay with them.

— Luke 24:28-29

"... they constrained him ..."

When the Lord appeared be "going further" as the disciples reached the village of Emmaus, the Gospel tells us that they "constrained him." The Greek word that is translated as "constrained" in the Revised Standard Version is a word that connotes violence or force.

This may shock us. But let us recall the scope of the story so far. Our Lord met the two disciples as they traveled to Emmaus. They were distraught at how the Lord had been treated at the hands of the worldly rulers. Our Lord in response to this rebuked them. He told them that they were slow to believe and that all these "things had to happen." Then He opened the Scriptures to them until they reached the village to which they were journeying. Then He "appears to be going further," and they "constrain" Him from doing so.

It is as if they had learned from His teaching on the road that God has willingly placed Himself into our hands. As in the Passion when our Lord was handed over to the rulers and did not fight His arrest, so now the Risen Lord is arrested by His disciples and made to stay with them.

If we reflect upon this and its meaning for us in this Mass, and indeed in the daily events of our lives, we will find that God has put Himself into "our hands." It is up to us to intercede and to mediate through Christ, who has handed Himself over to us for the needs and salvation of others.

OPPORTUNITY FOR SPIRITUAL GROWTH

Make a conscious effort daily to pray for the needs of the Church:

- **Pray for the Holy Father, your bishop, your pastor, and the other ministers in your parish.**

- **Pray for the government leaders in your country and in your community.**

- **Pray for your family members.**

- **Pray for anyone who has asked for your prayers.**

15

How to Join in the Preparation of the Gifts

CONTENTS OF THIS CHAPTER

- **The Liturgy of the Eucharist**
- **The Collection**
- **Preparation of the Altar**
- **Procession of the Gifts Hymn**
- **Procession of the Gifts**
- **Blessing the Bread and the Wine**
- **Hand Washing**
- **Our Offering**
- **Our Response**
- **Prayer Over the Gifts**
- **Meditation — "... he took the bread and blessed ..."**

THE LITURGY OF THE EUCHARIST

In the same way that the Mass begins with prayers to help us prepare to hear the Scriptures proclaimed in the Liturgy of the Word, so now we prepare to offer the Eucharistic sacrifice.

Our participation in the Liturgy of the Word was centered on opening ourselves fully to the Word of God proclaimed to us. Now we prepare ourselves to join our sacrifice with the sacrifice of our Lord Jesus Christ that is offered at this Mass.

Our Lord, on the night before He died, took bread and wine and instructed His apostles to do this in commemoration of Him. In this part of the Mass we bring the bread and wine to the altar. The priest will "take the bread" from the congregation and say the "blessing" over it. This will lead us into the next part of Mass, when we pray a great prayer of "giving thanks" (literally what "Eucharist" means), before the priest "breaks the bread" and "gives it to us" in communion.

Reflecting on this, Saint Paul told the Corinthians: "For as often as you eat this bread and drink the cup, you proclaim the Lord's death until he comes" (1 Corinthians 11:26).

Both bread and wine are made by gathering the many and crushing them into a unified substance. Crushing many grains of wheat and molding them into one substance makes bread. Crushing grapes into juice and letting the juice age and ferment makes wine. The Church, which is the Body of Christ, is made up of the "many," who are made one through the sacrifice of Jesus.

In the preparatory rites of the Liturgy of the Eucharist, we prepare to offer ourselves, along with the presider, to God the Father in union with the one sacrifice of Christ.

THE COLLECTION

In the early Church people would bring the bread and wine from their homes and present it to the presider during the Mass. Now the bread and wine are bought, but we still have the opportunity to "give" of ourselves at Mass.

One of the most concrete ways that we offer some part of ourselves in the Mass is by giving in the offertory collection. In most churches a basket is passed around, and we are presented with an opportunity to give of our hard-earned money. For better or worse, money has come to symbolize in our culture what really matters to us.

Giving in the collection is a symbolic but very real way of dying to ourselves. It proclaims that our faith is ultimately in God, not in our material wealth. Of course, it also pays the very real bills that the church accrues every time the lights, heat, or air conditioning are turned on. Most of us would be shocked to know how much it actually costs to pay such bills.

WHERE IS IT IN SCRIPTURE?

Examples of stewardship abound in Scripture. Here are several that specifically deal with the giving of money:

- Paying of the temple tax (Matthew 17:24-27)

- Widow's mite (Luke 21:1-4)

- Saint Paul's collection (1 Corinthians 16:1-4)

In the same way that our Lord handed Himself over to sinful men and was sacrificed on the cross for our salvation, we now give of ourselves, too. It is not to recreate His sacrifice, but rather to participate in His sacrifice. We will offer ourselves through Christ to the Father in the Eucharistic Prayer.

PREPARATION OF THE ALTAR

During the collection, the altar is prepared. The altar is the center of the Liturgy of the Eucharist, much in the same way that the ambo was the center of the Liturgy of the Word. Now the altar is readied, usually by the altar servers, although some parishes may have members of the congregation doing this. A corporal, purificator, Sacramentary, paten, and chalice are all placed on the altar.

WHAT ARE THEY?

CORPORAL A square linen cloth that the chalice and paten rest upon on the top of the altar.

PURIFICATOR A linen cloth used to clean the chalice.

SACRAMENTARY A book containing the various prayers said at Mass.

PATEN A sacred plate used to hold the bread that will be consecrated at Mass.

CHALICE A sacred cup used to hold the water and wine that will be consecrated at Mass.

PROCESSION OF THE GIFTS HYMN

A hymn is sung while the altar is being prepared and the gifts are being assembled. It continues as they are brought from the congregation to the presider of the Mass in a procession. Again, the hymn brings together all of us into one and is a way of unifying the action of those who represent us with ourselves.

PROCESSION OF THE GIFTS

A very important part of the preparation of the gifts to be offered at this Mass is the procession of the gifts. Remember that at the very beginning of the Mass, there was a procession in which the Book of the Gospels was held aloft as the various ministers entered the church building. Now there is another procession, this one involving representatives from the congregation.

How these representatives from the congregation are chosen varies from parish to parish. Many times an usher will approach a group of people and ask them to carry up the gifts. Sometimes if there is a family celebrating an important event, such as the baptism of a child or an anniversary, they will be selected. It doesn't matter how it is done, but it is important to understand the significance of people from the congregation bringing these gifts to the presider of the Mass.

The gifts represent us, and the people who bring them to the front emphasize the fact that "we" the congregation are asking the presider to take these gifts and to offer them to God in our name.

It is important because it sets the tone for us to understand that while the presider will say many of the prayers during this part of the Mass, he is saying them for all of us who are offering this Mass to God with him.

BLESSING THE BREAD AND THE WINE

Once the presider has been given the bread and wine, both are taken and placed on the altar. If a deacon is present, he will prepare the cup by pouring a drop of water into the wine (if there is no deacon, the priest will do this) while saying a prayer. His prayer requests that we who participate in this Mass may come to share in the divinity of Christ (symbolized by the wine) who humbled Himself to share in our humanity (symbolized by the drop of water).

The blessings said over the bread and the cup are derived from ancient Jewish prayers still in use today (see below) by those celebrating the Sabbath. Given the context of the Last Supper, it is likely that they are very close to what Jesus would have said, when the Scriptures tell us that "he took bread, and blessed" (Mark 14:22).

Sometimes these blessings over the bread and wine are said silently by the priest. If he says them aloud, we make his prayer

---

WHAT IS IT?

THE KIDDUSH Blessings said during Sabbath celebrations and other Jewish feasts for the bread and wine.

"Blessed are You, Lord our God, Ruler of the universe, Who brings forth bread from the earth."

"Blessed are You, Lord our God, Ruler of the universe, Who creates the fruit of the vine."

— *How to Run A Traditional Jewish Household,* pp. 72, 84

---

our own by responding, "Blessed be God forever," calling to mind the words of Saint Paul, in his letter to the Romans: "the Creator, who is blessed for ever" (Romans 1:25).

On some occasions the gifts are incensed after the blessing of the bread and wine. Incense is made up of grains of material that, when heated, melt and give off a fragrant odor. It has been used by almost every world religion as a way of designating the sacred and showing reverence to God.

HOW TO RECEIVE A BLESSING WITH INCENSE

 The priest and people are both incensed in recognition of the Presence of Christ in them — the priest because of his Holy Orders, the people because of the dignity they possess through their baptism.

When the deacon or server comes to the center aisle with the thurible (a device that carries hot embers and incense), he will bow to the congregation. This is what you should do:

- Stand.
- Bow back toward him (as a way of acknowledging him).
- Make the sign of the cross as he swings the thurible in your direction.
- Repeat the bow to him (as a way of thanking him).
- Sit.

The Psalmist proclaimed in Psalm 141:2, "Let my prayer be counted as incense before thee," and incense was ordered to be used in the Holy of Holies in Leviticus 16:12. The cloud of fragrant smoke reminds us that what we are doing is a very sacred act. When the bread and wine are incensed, the altar is also incensed, as well as the processional cross. A deacon or altar server incenses the priest, and then the congregation.

HAND WASHING

The priest next says two prayers quietly, but in these days of microphones most people usually have overheard them enough to know these prayers as well as the other prayers at Mass.

The first is a prayer of contrition. As he bows before the altar, the priest asks that the Lord would be pleased with "the sacrifice" that is being offered to Him, not out of pride but indeed out of humility and contrition.

The second prayer accompanies the "washing of the hands." This prayer usually calls to mind the Passion of our Lord and the act of Pontius Pilate before the crowd, but it is more an act of ritualizing the prayer of Psalm 51 that the priest says silently as he washes his hands:

> *"Wash me thoroughly from my iniquity,*
> *and cleanse me from my sin!"*
>
> — Psalm 51:2

OUR OFFERING

In some cases, as has been mentioned, the priest will have prayed all of the preceding prayers inaudibly. So it is quite possible that the first words we hear at any given Mass during the Liturgy of the Eucharist are an invitation by the priest to join him in prayer that God may accept his sacrifice and ours.

It is worth noting that in the priest's invitation to us is a plea that the sacrifice being offered to the Father will be acceptable. This presents us with a Biblical truth that in the Scriptures there are times when people offer an unacceptable sacrifice to God:

- In Genesis 4, God accepts the sacrifice offered by Abel, "but for Cain and his offering he had no regard" (Genesis 4:5).
- In Malachi 1:6-11, God rejects the sacrifice of the priests, saying, "I have no pleasure in you, says the LORD of hosts,

and I will not accept an offering from your hand" (Malachi 1:10). Malachi then goes on to prophesy what has traditionally been seen as a prophecy fulfilled in the celebration of the Mass and alluded to in the Third Eucharistic Prayer: "For from the rising of the sun to its setting my name is great among the nations, and in every place incense is offered in my name, and a pure offering" (Malachi 1:11).

- Saint Paul appeals to us in his Letter to the Romans to "present your bodies as a living sacrifice, holy and acceptable to God, which is your spiritual worship" (Romans 12:1).

CATHOLIC BELIEFS

A Mass intention may be attached to most Masses. This means that the priest is offering the Mass specifically for an intention someone has requested.

Does this mean that all the benefits of the Mass go to that one intention? The answer is no — every Mass benefits those in attendance and the entire Church, as well as the person or group who asked for a special remembrance at the Mass.

A person wishing to have Mass said for an individual or group usually can arrange to do so through the parish office at their church. It is customary to make an offering called a "stipend" when requesting a Mass intention. **The Code of Canon Law states,** "The Christian faithful who give an offering to apply the Mass for their intention contribute to the good of the Church and by that offering share its concern to support its ministers and works" **(Canon 946).**

OUR RESPONSE

We respond to the invitation of the presider by asking God to accept the sacrifice that we offer at the hands of the priest. We then ask for specific benefits from this sacrifice that is being offered. Specifically we ask:

— That the Lord accept this sacrifice

— For the praise of God's name

— For our good

— For the good of all God's people

It is good to spend a few moments reflecting on the posture of this response. We stand in response to the priest's invitation, but we approach God tentatively, asking Him to accept our sacrifice, for the praise of His name (as we are His creation), that it might be for our salvation and for the salvation of all.

It is a prayer we should say with much reflection.

PRAYER OVER THE GIFTS

All of these prayers are now gathered by the presider in a prayer that takes to heart the special circumstances of the day and asks God again to accept the gifts that we offer Him in faith through our Lord Jesus Christ.

We respond with an "Amen!"

MEDITATION

When [Jesus] was at table with them, he took the bread and blessed, and broke it, and gave it to them.

— Luke 24:30

"... he took the bread and blessed ..."

The disciples who still did not recognize our Lord now recline with Him at table. The words of the Gospel of Luke are interesting in light of what subsequently will happen. Luke says,

"So he went in to stay with them" (Luke 24:29). But in a few verses the same Gospel writer will proclaim that "he vanished out of their sight" (Luke 24:31). Is there a contradiction here, or is there a deeper meaning? Is not Saint Luke revealing a truth about how the Risen Lord was to "stay with us?"

It starts here, with Jesus taking bread, and blessing it — something that in and of itself would not have seemed strange in a culture where a blessing was always said over food that was to be eaten. Indeed we may miss out ourselves, by sometimes being too used to the ritual of the Mass and not noticing the momentous event that this simple start signifies.

May God enliven in us a deep sense of His desire to come and to "stay with us."

OPPORTUNITY FOR SPIRITUAL GROWTH

 Give of yourself at every Mass you attend. Be a good steward of all that God has given you:

- Use your voice to praise Him and answer the prayers meaningfully.

- Use your voice to sing with the congregation.

- Use your body to reverence God by genuflecting, standing, beating your breast, sitting, making the sign of the cross, bowing, and kneeling.

- Give generously in the collection, giving back to God's Church some of what you have received.

Truly offer yourself in union with Jesus to the Father, asking the Holy Spirit to help you!

16

How to Give Thanks to God in the Eucharistic Prayer

CONTENTS OF THIS CHAPTER

- **The Eucharistic Prayers**
- **The Preface**
- **The *Sanctus***
- **Kneeling**
- ***Epiclesis***
- **The Institutional Narrative and Consecration**
- **The *Anamnesis* (Memorial)**
- **The Mystery of Faith**
- **Intercessions**

THE EUCHARISTIC PRAYERS

"Eucharist" is a Greek word that means to "give thanks." The Eucharistic Prayer, also called the *anaphora* (a Greek word meaning "offering"), is the very heart of the Mass.

There are a number of Eucharistic Prayers that can be used by the priest at Mass. They all have a common form so that although they vary somewhat, there are key parts you will always recognize. These are:

- The Preface (which includes the "Holy, Holy, Holy")
- The *epiclesis* (the invocation of the Holy Spirit)
- The Institutional Narrative
- The *anamnesis* (memorial)
- The intercessions
- The Great Doxology

We will explain each of these parts in this chapter, so don't worry if some of the words seem strange to you — even if you've been Catholic your whole life.

THE PREFACE

This great prayer of thanksgiving and consecration begins with a "Preface." Most of us are familiar with a preface at the beginning of a book, but probably not in prayer. But then there is no prayer quite like this prayer, in which our Lord changes bread and wine into His Flesh and Blood.

The Preface is ancient. It goes all the way back to the early Church when Christianity was still a sect within Judaism. Most of the elements of the prayer, including the "Holy, Holy, Holy" were part of a prayer said every morning in the synagogue.

In the fourth century, Saint Cyril of Jerusalem, in his *Catechetical Lectures*, mentions two parts of this prayer that may be the most confusing to the modern-day pray-er at Mass. His comments in the box below may give you new insight on how the Preface prepares us for the rest of the Eucharistic Prayer.

THE FAITH OF THE EARLY CHURCH

Saint Cyril's commentary on "Lift up your hearts":

"The priest cries out: 'Lift up your hearts!' For in this most solemn hour it is necessary for us to have our hearts raised up with God, and not fixed below, on the earth and earthly things. It is as if the priest instructs us at this hour to dismiss all physical cares and domestic anxieties, and to have our hearts in heaven with the benevolent God. Then you answer: 'We have lifted them up to the Lord,' giving assent to it by the acknowledgment that you make. Let no one come here, then, who could say with his mouth, 'We have lifted them up to the Lord,' while he is preoccupied with physical cares."

— *Catechetical Lectures* 848d, Saint Cyril of Alexandria, A.D. 350

The priest begins by invoking the Lord's Presence upon us, and we in return ask the Lord to be with him. Then he tells us to lift up our hearts. Notice Cyril's comment on this. If at the beginning of the liturgy we are weighed down with our earthly cares, the Preface now asks us to set them aside. Lifting up our hearts means transcending the present difficulties and joining the heavenly liturgy, where all our troubles will vanish in the twinkling of an eye.

We may have responded to the Preface by replying that we have lifted our hearts without ever understanding what we were supposed to be doing. Reread Cyril's commentary and try to practice this the next time you go to Mass: to at this moment consciously set aside all of your concerns for the period of this prayer and just focus on God intensely.

THE FAITH OF THE EARLY CHURCH

Saint Cyril's Commentary on "Let us give thanks to the Lord":

"Then the priest says, 'Let us give thanks to the Lord.' Certainly we ought to give thanks to God for having invited us, unworthy as we are, to so great a gift; for God having reconciled us to Himself when we were His enemies; for having made us His adopted sons by the Spirit. Then you say, 'It is right and just': for in giving thanks, we do a worthy thing, something that is justice itself. But what God did in accounting us worthy of such benefits was not justice, but much more than just."

— *Catechetical Lectures* 848e, Saint Cyril of Alexandria, A.D. 350

Next we are invited to participate fully in this prayer of thanksgiving by doing just that, giving thanks to God. Again Cyril's commentary points out that if we are really mindful of all that God has done for us, we know that we owe God everything, including our very existence.

The prayer of the Preface continues as the priest gives thanks to God the Father, listing the many works of the Father that we experience in the world He has created, the sending of His Son and the Holy Spirit for our redemption and sanctification. If you listen to the prayer you will find that this thanks is modified depending upon what is being celebrated in the Church calendar.

One way of thinking of this prayer is to remember someone who has so much to thank someone for that he keeps listing the reasons — you did this for me, and you did this for me, and as though that weren't enough you even did this for me. The Preface builds up to a joining with all the heavenly hosts (whom we have joined because we've lifted our hearts up to heaven) and singing with them their song of praise.

THE *SANCTUS*

Sanctus is the Latin word for "holy." The more accurate name of this prayer is the Latin *Tersanctus*, meaning "three holies," which is apparent because "holy" is repeated three times at the very beginning of the prayer.

Our response to all of the great things that God has done for us is to first join in with the heavenly choir and sing a passage found both in Isaiah and the Book of Revelation (see "Where is it in Scripture?" below). Then we join in with those who welcomed our Lord as He entered the city of Jerusalem on Palm Sunday.

WHERE IS IT IN SCRIPTURE?

The *Sanctus* is derived from several different passages in the Bible:

"Holy, holy, holy is the Lᴏʀᴅ of hosts;
    the whole earth is full of his glory."

— Isaiah 6:3

"Holy, holy, holy, is the Lord God Almighty...." — Revelation 4:8

"Hosanna! Blessed is he who comes in the name of the Lord! ... Hosanna in the highest!" — Mark 11:9-10

(emphasis added)

Knowing where the parts of the *Sanctus* (Latin for "Holy") come from in Scripture should help us to reflect on what is going on here. The quotes from Isaiah and the Book of Revelation relate the worship of God in heaven. The quote from the Gospel relates to the worship of God on earth — Jesus the Son of God entering Jerusalem, where He would celebrate the Last Supper, be crucified, die, and rise again from the dead.

Here we are on earth joining the worship of God in heaven and celebrating that He has chosen to become one of us. This is a song of great praise to God both for what He has done and is about to do during this Mass.

HOW TO KNEEL

Drop to both knees, resting your weight on them. Fold your hands in a prayerful posture and focus on God.

KNEELING

At the end of the "Holy, Holy, Holy," you will kneel. This change in our posture further emphasizes what the Preface has already brought out, that we are to set our focus on God. Kneeling has the effect, perhaps because our weight is shifted to our knees, of changing our level of attention. Where sitting may help us to listen, kneeling seems to require something more sacrificial and active from us.

WHAT DOES IT MEAN? ──────────

The posture of kneeling during prayer communicates:

- **Adoration (something that is given to God alone)**

- **Repentance (for anything that we allow to take our focus off God)**

- **Submission (to the will of God)**

EPICLESIS

Epiclesis is a Greek word that means to "invoke upon." The first *epiclesis* during the Eucharistic Prayer asks God the Father to send His Holy Spirit upon the gifts of bread and wine so that they may become for us the Body and Blood of our Lord.

In all of the Eucharistic Prayers, the action of the priest during this *epiclesis* over the bread and wine is the same. He places his hands, palms down, over the bread and wine as he says the prayer, then makes a sign of the cross over them with his right hand.

In the Eastern Churches, this is the moment at which they believe that the bread and wine become the Body and Blood of our Lord. But in the Roman Catholic Church (the West), it is believed that it is at the moment when the priest says the words of institution.

There is a second part to the *epiclesis* that invokes the Spirit again, asking that all who share in the Body and Blood of Christ may be brought together in unity to themselves become one body, one spirit in Christ. We should not let the richness of this action pass us by — that by receiving the Body and Blood of Christ we become part of the one Body of Christ.

THE INSTITUTIONAL NARRATIVE AND CONSECRATION

The institutional narrative is a retelling of what Jesus did "on the night before he died," but it is more than just a telling — it is a making present. As the priest recites the words, we are brought to the presence of the event that Jesus attached to the Last Supper — His death on the cross at Calvary.

As the priest recites the words of the institution of the Eucharist, he recounts what Jesus did at the Last Supper, drawing from all the Scriptural accounts of it. Here the Word of God is efficacious — it has the power to bring about through the Holy Spirit what it says; the words of Jesus bring about the reality.

The consecration is the moment when the bread and wine become the Body and Blood of Christ. This happens when the priest recites the words of Jesus over them.

He takes the bread into his hands, repeats what Jesus did and says what He said: "This is my body, which will be given up for you."

The priest, after elevation of the bread, places it back on the altar and genuflects in adoration of the Lord now present in the sacred species.

He then takes the cup and says the words of institution, similar to "This cup is the new covenant in my blood. Do this, as often as you drink it, in remembrance of me," from 1 Corinthians 11:25. He then elevates the chalice, and he then sets down the chalice. And again genuflects in adoration.

The way that the bread and wine are consecrated separately — first the bread becomes our Lord's Body, then the wine becomes His Blood — symbolizes the Lord's death on the cross. Later in the Mass, the Body and Blood of our Lord are brought together, in the Mingling Rite, so that what we receive at Holy Communion is the Risen Lord.

THE *ANAMNESIS* (MEMORIAL)

When Jesus told His disciples to "Do this in memory of me," He was speaking of "memory" in the Jewish sense. For the Jews to do something in memorial meant to make "present" the event.

So during the Passover celebration, a child would ask his father, "Why is this night different than all the others?" — The "night of the Passover" is made present.

This is true as well for the Eucharist. We are present at Calvary. This is hinted at in the Book of Revelation, which describes the liturgy of the Mass in heaven. There the "Lamb who was slain" is present; this is the Lamb of God — Jesus.

The offering of the bread and wine that become the Body and Blood of Christ during the Eucharistic Prayer is a presentation of the one sacrifice of Christ on Calvary. By our participation we share in this sacrifice, which is not a "new" sacrifice but the one sacrifice that Christ performed when He was both the priest (the one presenting the offering) and victim (what was offered).

The memorial is a part of the Eucharistic Prayer that recalls to God the Father the sacrifice of His Son, Jesus, who has ransomed

"We carry out this command of the Lord by celebrating the *memorial of His sacrifice*. In so doing, *we offer to the Father* what he has himself given us: the gifts of his creation, bread and wine which, by the power of the Holy Spirit and by the words of Christ, have become the body and blood of Christ. Christ is thus really and mysteriously made *present*."

— *CCC*, No. 1357

"The Eucharistic Presence of Christ begins at the moment of the consecration and endures as long as the Eucharistic species subsist. Christ is present whole and entire in each of the species and whole and entire in each of their parts, in such a way that the breaking of the bread does not divide Christ."

— *CCC*, No. 1377

"283. What is the meaning of *transubstantiation*?
Transubstantiation means the change of the whole substance of bread into the substance of the Body of Christ and of the whole substance of wine into the substance of his Blood. This change is brought about in the eucharistic prayer through the efficacy of the word of Christ and by the action of the Holy Spirit. However, the outward characteristics of bread and wine, that is the 'eucharistic species,' remain unaltered."

— *Compendium*, No.283

us. After the consecration we remind God of His love for the Son and His love for us.

THE MYSTERY OF FAITH

After the consecration, the people are invited to acclaim the "mystery of faith." This simple acclamation proclaims belief in the Resurrection of the Lord whose death we have just mystically witnessed. We acknowledge the reality of His death in this simple acclamation, but we also proclaim our faith that He is alive and that He will come again.

INTERCESSIONS

The Mass is celebrated in union with the whole Church (all who have lived and died in Christ, both in heaven and on earth), and this is made explicit in the Eucharistic Prayers. The members of the Church are remembered in prayer; some by name, such as the pope and the bishop of the diocese where the Mass is celebrated, and some more generally.

If Eucharistic Prayer I is prayed, there are two places at which the priest will stop and allow us to silently include the names of those we wish to pray for personally. The first time occurs before the consecration and is for those who are living whom we wish to pray for. The second time occurs after the consecration and is for those who have died whom we wish to remember in prayer. We should silently make whatever Eucharistic Prayer is prayed at Mass our own by praying along with the priest silently and attentively.

OPPORTUNITY FOR SPIRITUAL GROWTH

Make the prayer of the priest your own.

Adore the Lord in a special way by making an act of reverence at the consecration.

Pray for the whole Church and add your own intentions, too.

17

How to Say "Amen" to the Eucharistic Prayer

CONTENTS OF THIS CHAPTER

- The Doxology
- The Great Amen
- The Assent of the Faithful
- Making the Amen Our Own

THE DOXOLOGY

A doxology is a Greek word that means "a word of praise." If you have ever had the opportunity to attend prayer in a Catholic monastery and were unfamiliar with that type of prayer, you may have been surprised when at the end of the chanting of every Psalm the monks rose, then bowed at the waist and chanted the Glory Be. What they were doing reflects an ancient practice in which prayers were always ended by recalling the supreme purpose of prayer — the creature bowing before the Creator and singing His praises.

Every Eucharistic Prayer ends in this way, with a great doxology singing praise to God. The priest raises the Body and Blood of Christ, presenting them to the Father as he says or sings that it is "through him, with him, and in him." The "him" is Jesus, now present in the consecrated bread and wine.

God the Father is offered the Son through the power of the Holy Spirit that animates the Church. This is the culmination of the Eucharistic Prayer. All of us are presented to God the Father through the Son, unified by the Holy Spirit.

THE FAITH OF THE EARLY CHURCH

"When the presider has concluded the prayers and thanksgivings, all present give voice to an acclamation by saying: 'Amen.'"

— Saint Justin Martyr, A.D. 155

THE GREAT AMEN

We now acclaim the "Great Amen." It is so important because the prayer that has both made our Lord present and offered Him in sacrifice to the Father is great. Saint Augustine said that "Amen is the people's signature." In this amen, we don't merely sign our name, we leave our John Hancock.

Usually the Great Amen is sung, and repeated a number of times in a joyous manner to emphasize that we give our assent to the prayer over and over. If we reflect upon our great need for a savior and what a great savior we have in Jesus, who is now present in the bread and wine, we cannot help but be joyous and thankful as we sing our Great Amen.

WHERE IS IT IN SCRIPTURE?

"And the four living creatures said, 'Amen!' and the elders fell down and worshiped."

— Revelation 5:14

THE ASSENT OF THE FAITHFUL

We have remained kneeling for the Eucharistic Prayer; now we stand. The movement usually happens almost instantaneously with the singing of the amen. It is as though the congregation cannot contain themselves but must rise to give their assent to the prayer that the priest has prayed in their name.

Even if "Amen" is said only once, we should be mindful of its nature and importance.

MAKING THE AMEN OUR OWN

It is easy when we have attended Mass for many years to lose sight of the importance of our "amen" to all that Jesus means to us. We should always meditate on what a difference our Lord makes. Saints have meditated on their final end to keep before them the great need that we have for a savior, someone who can rescue us from death.

Whatever it takes, you should not allow this to become routine. When it does, it is a good indication that you need to rekindle the fire of the love of God in your life.

We often say yes in a way that reflects that we really don't mean it. We often sign our name to documents that we haven't fully read. Don't let this happen at Mass. Actively and fully let your "yes," your "AMEN," mean it!

Then let this flow over into your daily life in all that you say "yes" to and in all that you sign your name to, in all that you give your "Amen!"

18

—— How to Pray the Lord's Prayer ——

CONTENTS OF THIS CHAPTER

- Praying as Jesus Taught
- "Our Father, who art in heaven"
- "Hallowed be thy name"
- "Thy kingdom come"
- "Thy will be done on earth as it is in heaven"
- "Give us this day our daily bread"
- "Forgive us our trespasses as we forgive"
- "And lead us not into temptation"
- "But deliver us from evil"
- Deliver Us, Lord
- For the Kingdom

PRAYING AS JESUS TAUGHT

In acknowledging that Jesus is "our way" to the Father, we immediately turn our gaze to Jesus and the way He instructed His disciples to pray. The Our Father was prayed by the early Christians and continues to be a prayer said by all Christians. The *Didache*, which is quoted at the beginning of this chapter, instructed the Christians of the second century to pray the Our Father three times daily.

Some aspects of the Our Father may not be clear to us who pray it today. The early Christians were convinced that Jesus was coming back to establish the kingdom of God soon. He had told His disciples that they could not know the day nor the hour, but He had counseled them to ever be alert and ready, for He would come "like a thief in the night" when they least expected Him. The early followers were aware of Jesus' command and prayed for His coming.

Each celebration of the Mass was an intense time of praying for our Lord to come again, and it still is (although this may be lost on us). The oldest Christian prayers, such as the simple prayer *Maranatha* — "Come, Lord" — and the Our Father, pray for the Lord to come again. In the petitions that make up the Our Father, we are praying that all obstacles be removed from our lives so we might have perfect communion with God and with our brothers and sisters. The following commentary on this prayer draws heavily on the work of the late Father Raymond Brown. His treatment of the Lord's Prayer can be found in *New Testament Essays* (see "Where Can I Learn More?" on Page 261).

"OUR FATHER, WHO ART IN HEAVEN"

Jesus called God "my father," and He instructs us to call God "our Father," which is possible because of our relationship to Jesus. The prayer locates "our Father" in heaven. Our eyes are

---

— WHERE IS IT IN SCRIPTURE? —

The Lord's Prayer is found in both the Gospel of Matthew and Luke. The way it has been traditionally prayed most closely matches Matthew's version:

"Our Father who art in heaven,
Hallowed be thy name.
Thy kingdom come.
Thy will be done,
On earth as it is in heaven.
Give us this day our daily bread;
And forgive us our debts,
As we also have forgiven our debtors;
And lead us not into temptation,
But deliver us from evil."

— Matthew 6:9-13

Luke's version of the Our Father is found in Luke 11:2-4.

---

to be on our home where "our Father" dwells. In fact, the entire prayer that Jesus taught us points to the culmination and the coming of the heavenly kingdom where the reign of Christ will be complete.

Already this Mass prefigures the heavenly banquet.

"HALLOWED BE THY NAME"

Remembering that this prayer is addressed to God the Father helps us to understand what we are asking God to do here. We are asking God to manifest the holiness of His name to all people. Remember that in the Gospel of John, Jesus prayed, "Father, glorify thy name" (John 12:28). Jesus' prayer is answered immediately when the Father answers from the heavens, "I have glorified it, and I will glorify it again" (John 12:28).

In response to this petition of the Our Father, we have the great things that God has done in the past that have made His name great, what He has done for us during this Mass, and all that He has promised to do for us.

"THY KINGDOM COME"

The establishment of the kingdom of God began with the coming of Jesus, but it has not yet reached its fulfillment when everything shall be subject to Him. Recall that in Jesus' temptations, Satan told our Lord that the earthly kingdoms had been "delivered" to him. The First Letter of John says, "We know that we are of God, and the whole world is in the power of the evil one" (1 John 5:19).

When Jesus spoke of His Second Coming in Luke 21, He told His disciples, "when you see these things taking place, you know that the kingdom of God is near" (Luke 21:31). So in this petition of the Our Father we pray that God will bring His kingdom to fulfillment in our midst.

"THY WILL BE DONE ON EARTH AS IT IS IN HEAVEN"

"Will" has several meanings in Scripture. There is our will (what we want to do), and then there is God's "will" (God's supreme plan). Jesus in His agony in the garden prayed to the Father that His "will" be done. We know that ultimately God's will is to be accomplished on earth as it is perfectly in heaven. But because of sin (acts that separate us from God) and evil in the world, God's will is not done perfectly.

Again this petition of the Our Father is asking God to bring about the establishment of His reign over the earth. The earth is described as a "paradise" before our first parents disregarded God's will. Jesus came to re-establish God's kingdom, but the full establishment of God's reign will occur when Jesus comes again as judge. Each time we pray the Our Father, we are asking God to allow Jesus to come now.

"GIVE US THIS DAY OUR DAILY BREAD"

This petition that again is addressed to God the Father reminds us of what God did for the Israelites in the desert. The Psalmist says, "They asked, and he brought quails, and gave them bread from heaven in abundance" (Psalm 105:40). It also recalls what Jesus did when He fed the multitudes by multiplying the loaves of bread and fishes. We are asking here that God give us "heavenly bread," the food that is served at the heavenly banquet.

Of course, this petition is soon to be answered for us. It is interesting to note that at a certain time in their Christian formation, the catechumens will be presented with the Our Father, as well as the creed. The Church withholds both until the catechumens are close to the point when at least this part of the prayer will be answered for them.

One of those who heard Jesus teach cried out, "Blessed is he who shall eat bread in the kingdom of God!" (Luke 14:15). We are those who are "blessed" that this petition is answered by God for us at this Mass.

"FORGIVE US OUR TRESPASSES AS WE FORGIVE"

There is an urgency in the petitions of the Our Father as they appear in the original language of Scripture that does not translate well into English. This petition for forgiveness "as we forgive" is really a call for instant forgiveness — to be forgiven right at this moment.

Again there is a tie-in with the Second Coming of Jesus. The early Christians believed that Christ could come at any moment (this is still the belief of the Church, I should add), and that when He did, He would come as judge. So forgiveness of sins was of the utmost urgency, because Christ could come at this very moment to render the Father's judgment.

But when Jesus taught this prayer to His disciples, He added "as we forgive," reminding His disciples that they should expect the Father to forgive as they themselves forgave. One has only to remember the Parable of the Unforgiving Servant in Matthew 18:23-35, in which our Lord concludes with, "And in anger his lord delivered him to the jailers, till he should pay all his debt. So also my heavenly Father will do to every one of you, if you do not forgive your brother from your heart" (Matthew 18:34-35).

There is in this one petition of the Our Father both an "act of contrition" and "examination of conscience," while at the same time a meditation on the final judgment.

"AND LEAD US NOT INTO TEMPTATION"

This final petition of the Our Father is probably the least understood. One might commonly think that we are asking God not to "tempt" us. But Christians familiar with the Bible would see that this is not the case: We find in the Letter of James: "Let no one say when he is tempted, 'I am tempted by God'; for God cannot be tempted with evil and he himself tempts no one; but each person is tempted when he is lured and enticed by his own desire" (James 1:13-14).

The problem may be that the word translated as "temptation" in the English version of the Our Father is probably better translated "trial." It is the same Greek word that is used in the Book of Revelation when our Lord says, "Because you have kept my word of patient endurance, I will keep you from the hour of trial which is coming on the whole world, to try those who dwell upon the earth" (Revelation 3:10).

This "hour of trial" is the final battle between good and evil. Obviously, the early Christians faced persecution from human hands, but what is envisioned here is an all-out spiritual war joined to a physical war against the Body of Christ, the Church. There was the belief that Satan had a certain period in which to tempt those on earth, and that when that time grew short, he would unleash a battle the likes of which had never been experienced by anyone on earth. Jesus told His disciples to pray that they might not be subjected to that horrible period.

"BUT DELIVER US FROM EVIL"

The final petition asks that the Lord "deliver us from evil." Again what the English translation gives as "evil" is more literally "the evil," which was one of the biblical names for Satan. We ask God in the first that we not be subjected to the final battle between good and evil, and then that we be delivered from all the works of Satan.

In Scripture we find Jesus praying for His disciples: "I do not pray that thou shouldst take them out of the world, but that thou shouldst keep them from the *evil one*" (John 17:15, emphasis added). Saint Paul when addressing the Thessalonians says, "But the Lord is faithful; he will strengthen you and guard you from the evil one" (2 Thessalonians 3:3, NRSV).

DELIVER US, LORD

The prayer that follows the Our Father is said by the priest. In some ways this prayer emphasizes the Church's own continuing plea that the Father will deliver us from all evil and grant us peace.

This prayer renews the sense that in the Lord's Prayer we are praying for the coming of Christ. Indeed, He will come to us in the Eucharistic species that we are soon to receive; but we also pray for Him to come to establish the kingdom of God fully upon the earth.

The prayer hints at the Gospel of Luke and Jesus' teaching on how His disciples should react to His Second Coming. While the nonbelievers are dying of fear for what is overtaking the world, Jesus tells His disciples, "Now when these things begin to take place, look up and raise your heads, because your redemption is drawing near" (Luke 21:28). The establishment of God's kingdom is a joyful event that all Christians look forward to and pray will happen soon.

FOR THE KINGDOM

We respond not with an "amen" in this instance, but rather with an ancient prayer found in the *Didache* and in some (but not all) ancient manuscripts of Scripture. It is a prayer expressing faith in God and how right it is for us to put all of our trust in Him.

We spoke in the previous chapter about "doxologies," about the custom of summing up prayers by singing the glories of God. This is another way of doing just that. The *Didache* says it simply: "For thine is the power and the glory forever."

Other Christian Churches pray this doxology at the end of the Our Father, but Catholics have always prayed it in the way that it is presented in the Scriptures. In Saint Cyril of Alexandria's commentary on the Our Father, found in his *Catechetical Lectures*, which are dated A.D. 350, he stops with "But deliver us from evil," saying: "Then, after the prayer has been completed, you say, 'Amen.' "

OPPORTUNITY FOR SPIRITUAL GROWTH

 Make a conscious effort to pray the Our Father with the meaning presented in the commentary in this chapter. Try to feel the urgency of pleading for the coming of God's kingdom in your life, when God's reign will be complete and all suffering will cease.

19

—— How to Give the Sign of Peace ——

CONTENTS OF THIS CHAPTER

- **Grant Us the Peace and Unity of Your Kingdom**
- **My Peace I Give You!**
- **Sharing Peace**

GRANT US THE PEACE AND UNITY OF YOUR KINGDOM

The priest prays a prayer out loud to Jesus, reminding Him of His gift of peace to the apostles. He then asks the Lord to look down upon the faith of the people gathered in this church and to grant us His peace and unity.

The prayer, coming as it does before Communion, reflects our need to be reconciled with one another. Receiving the Eucharist is a sign that we are in "communion with the Lord." Being in communion with the Lord means that we:

1. Accept Jesus as our Lord, have confessed and repented of our sins, and put our total trust in Him.
2. Accept the teachings of the Catholic Church that Jesus founded by making Peter the Apostle the head of the Church and giving him full power to forgive and bind sins.
3. Are at peace with our brothers and sisters.

The first two senses of "communion" have been experienced in the Penitential Rite and the Profession of Faith. Now we deal with the third in a concrete manner. We cannot be in communion with Jesus if we are not at peace with our brothers and sisters. "If any one says, 'I love God,' and hates his brother, he is a liar; for he who does not love his brother whom he has seen, cannot love God whom he has not seen" (1 John 4:20).

MY PEACE I GIVE YOU!

The priest, having finished the prayer in the Presence of Jesus in the Eucharistic species before him, now turns his gaze to us and from the altar offers us the peace of Jesus Christ. What will we do with it?

Mindful that within our families and workplaces and among our acquaintances people can and do cause us hurt and unrest, it goes without saying that we can use the Lord's peace. It is given to us freely. We should open our hearts to it, making this presentation a real encounter with Jesus' peace given to us.

Like anything that God gives us, it is too much for us alone. We immediately share it with the priest by asking the Lord to give him peace also.

WHERE IS IT IN SCRIPTURE?

The exchange of peace is an important precursor to our encounter with Jesus in Holy Communion, as is shown in the following Scripture passages:

"So if you are offering your gift at the altar, and there remember that your brother has something against you, leave your gift there before the altar and go; first be reconciled to your brother, and then come and offer your gift."   — Matthew 5:23-24

"Greet one another with a holy kiss."
—1 Corinthians 16:20, 2 Corinthians 13:12, Romans 16:16

"Greet all the brethren with a holy kiss."
— 1 Thessalonians 5:26

SHARING PEACE

The priest or deacon now invites us to share the Lord's peace with one another. In the United States, the usual way this is done is by a handshake. But the Catholic Church leaves this up to local custom, so if you are a world traveler you may find that in some places people embrace you at this point or even kiss you on the cheek. But exchanging the sign of peace should be just that — peaceful. It is not a time to lose our focus on the Lord Jesus; in fact, we should at this moment reverence the Lord who can come to us in the form of the stranger next to us.

OPPORTUNITY FOR SPIRITUAL GROWTH

Never allow the sign of peace to become an opportunity for tumult. Also beware of making a show of peace: Respect people's boundaries and what they are comfortable with. Make the sign of peace truly peaceful!

There are some who refuse to give the sign of peace. They will stare stone-faced straight ahead during its exchange. One never knows what their reason for doing so may be, but whatever it is, do not refuse them the peace that the Lord has given you. Offer a prayer on their behalf.

If you are sick or have a cold, it is prudent to tell those around you at the sign of peace and to wish them peace at the same time. This ritual isn't meant to force anyone to spread his or her germs, but rather to spread the Lord's peace and to show in action that we are a unity of His Presence.

20

How to Witness the Breaking of the Bread

CONTENTS OF THIS CHAPTER

- **The Breaking of the Bread**
- **Lamb of God ...**
- **Beating Your Breast?**
- **By This Mingling ...**
- **Meditation — "... and broke it ..."**

THE BREAKING OF THE BREAD

Immediately after the sign of peace is exchanged, the priest begins to break the Eucharistic bread. This is one of the key actions of Jesus, who took the bread, said the blessing (gave thanks), *broke it*, and gave it to His disciples. In the early Church, where one loaf of unleavened bread was used, the bread was broken so that everyone might partake. In later centuries the Church began using "hosts" already cut from a sheet ready-made for Communion. Unfortunately, the symbolism was lost in the process.

It is still retained in the breaking of the priest's host (which is larger) and, depending upon the parish where you attend Mass, a large unleavened loaf may even be broken. Because of the size of modern parishes this can create problems — I once attended a Mass in which the "breaking of the bread" took twenty minutes. In 2004, the Congregation for Divine Worship and the Discipline of the Sacraments pointed out in *Redemptionis Sacramentum* ("Instruction on the Eucharist") that the rite of breaking the bread should be brief and not given undue emphasis (No. 73).

THE FAITH OF THE EARLY CHURCH

"As the broken bread was scattered on the mountains, but brought together was made one, so gather your Church from the ends of the earth into your kingdom."

— *Didache*, A.D. 110

LAMB OF GOD ...

While the Eucharistic bread is being broken and the Precious Blood of Jesus is being poured into the chalices, we sing or say the "Lamb of God." In most parishes, "Lamb of God, who take away the sins of the world," is repeated twice with the response

"Have mercy on us," and a third time with the response "Grant us peace."

However, because the "Lamb of God" accompanies the breaking of the bread, it can go on for as long as that action takes. No matter how many times it is said, the final response is always "Grant us peace."

BEATING YOUR BREAST?

You may notice that some people beat their breast as they say this prayer. Before the new order of the Mass came into being in the 1960s, this symbolic gesture was used while saying the "Lamb of God." While the new rite doesn't call for this action to be done anytime other than during the *Confiteor*, it is appropriate to call to mind why this action was associated with this prayer and the one said right before Communion: "Lord, I am not worthy."

If we recall Jesus' teaching on true prayer, we will be struck by a reality: that our stance toward God is always that "we have sinned." It is the protocol of heaven, as it were, to always present ourselves to God in this fashion. We are never to be like the Pharisee, who thanks God that he is not like other men; but rather we are to imitate the tax collector, of whom Jesus says, "This man went down to his house justified rather than the other"

(Luke 18:14). We imitate the tax collector by truthfully acknowledging that we are sinners.

We should always approach our Lord in the utmost humility, even when He has blessed us richly with His graces. We should always remember that we are sinners in desperate need of Him to save us. Pride is the greatest obstacle to God's free gift of grace, because if we start feeling that we are "okay," we are less apt to see ourselves as in need of a savior and open ourselves to Him.

BY THIS MINGLING ...

The priest will do something that may be imperceptible to our eyes if we are not specifically looking for it. He will break off a small piece of the Eucharistic bread and drop it into the chalice that contains the Precious Blood of Jesus while he says a prayer silently. This is the "co-mingling" of the Body and Blood of Christ. It is a small act, but rich in symbolism.

First, it symbolizes the Resurrection of our Lord. At the consecration our Lord came to the bread and wine separately — this is my Body, this is my Blood; symbolic of His death on the cross. Now the two are joined.

Second, it symbolizes the unity of the Church. In the early Church a piece of the Eucharist from the Pope's Mass was broken off and taken to other churches and mingled with their Eucharistic species to signify that they were all one Body of Christ. This piece was called the *fermentum*, a Latin word that means leaven.

Third, in some parts of the Church it became the custom to retain this broken Eucharistic bread soaked in the Precious Blood for the Communion of the sick and dying. Obviously, given in this condition it would be easier for someone having difficulty in swallowing to partake in the Eucharist.

The prayer said by the priest as he performs this action asks that this action might "bring eternal life" to all who receive this Eucharist.

MEDITATION

"When he was at table with them, he took the bread and blessed, and broke it, and gave it to them."

— Luke 24:30

"... and broke it ..."

When the disciples invited our Lord to stay with them upon reaching Emmaus and sat down with Him at table, they still did not recognize Him. But when He took the bread, said the blessing and broke it, suddenly, Saint Luke tells us, "their eyes were opened and they recognized him" (Luke 24:31). Later, when they reported to the apostles what they had experienced, they described "how he was known to them in the breaking of the bread" (Luke 24:35), and as they said this, "Jesus himself stood among them" (Luke 24:36).

Jesus Himself stands in our midst. This is the moment of decision for each of us. Will our eyes open to His Presence? Are we blind to what we are about to partake in? Has our ability to receive Him so freely dulled our senses?

As you witness the "breaking of the bread," try to meditate on the Lord's Presence before you:

- Think of how the first disciples walked with Jesus but did not know it was Him.

- Think of how He opened the Scriptures to them, and how the events of their lives suddenly began to take on new meaning.
- Think of how they reached a spot in the road where it appeared that He would leave them but they begged Him to stay.
- Think of how their eyes were opened when He took the bread, said the blessing, and broke it.
- Ask the Lord to open your eyes to the miracle of His Presence in the bread and wine that have been offered at this Mass.
- Ask our Lord to open your eyes to the miracle of His Presence in the bread and wine that have been offered at this Mass.

OPPORTUNITY FOR SPIRITUAL GROWTH

Make acts of faith in the Real Presence of Jesus.

Silently pray the prayer of Saint Thomas, "My Lord and my God!" **(John 20:28). If you struggle with belief in the Eucharist, pray,** "I believe; help my unbelief!" **(Mark 9:24).**

21

How to Receive
Holy Communion

CONTENTS OF THIS CHAPTER

- Behold the Lamb of God ...
- Our Response
- Preparation to Receive the Eucharist
- Processing to the Altar
- Receiving the Eucharist
- Contemplating the Fruits of Holy Communion
- Prayer After Communion
- Meditation — "And their eyes were opened ..."

"Let us, then, with full confidence, partake of the Body and Blood of Christ. For in the appearance of bread His Body is given to you, and in the appearance of wine His Blood is given to you, so that partaking of the Body and Blood of Christ, you might become united in body and blood with Him. For thus do we become Christ-bearers, His Body and Blood being distributed through our members. And thus it is that we become, according to blessed Peter, sharers of the divine nature."

— Saint Cyril of Jerusalem, A.D. 350

BEHOLD THE LAMB OF GOD ...

The priest raises the Blessed Sacrament and, presenting Jesus to us, uses words from Scripture. He declares that this is the "Lamb of God" and how blessed are we who are invited to partake in His supper.

OUR RESPONSE

We respond to this invitation by declaring that we are unworthy. We use words directly from the Scriptures. They recall the

---
WHERE IS IT IN SCRIPTURE?

The first part of what he says are the words of Saint John the Baptist, who said to his disciples when he spotted Jesus:

"Behold, the Lamb of God, who takes away the sin of the world!" — John 1:29

The second part of what the priest says is from the Book of Revelation:

"And the angel said to me, 'Write this: Blessed are those who are invited to the marriage supper of the Lamb.' " — Revelation 19:9

---

words of the Roman centurion who sent his servants to summon Jesus to heal his slave. Before Jesus can arrive at the centurion's house, the man again sends his servants to deliver a message protesting that he is not worthy to have Jesus enter his house, but has faith that Jesus can command from afar and whatever Jesus commands will be done.

WHERE IS IT IN SCRIPTURE?

"Lord, I am not worthy," is taken from the Gospel of Luke:

"When he [Jesus] was not far from the house, the centurion sent friends to him, saying to him, "*Lord*, do not trouble yourself, for *I am not worthy to have you come under my roof*, therefore I did not presume to come to you. *But say the word, and* let *my* servant *be healed*." — Luke 7:6-7

(emphasis added)

The Church replaces "servant" with "soul," making the plea of the centurion for his servant now a plea that we make for ourselves. This prayer is a great example of how at Mass when we pray we are also "speaking" the Bible.

It is a remarkable testimony of faith, and we should be mindful of it as we say the words, slightly modified, ourselves. If we don't possess the faith of the centurion, we should ask the Lord to give it to us!

PREPARATION TO RECEIVE THE EUCHARIST

Remember that receiving the Eucharist at Mass is a gift of Christ. The Church wishes for all who attend Mass to receive Communion, but it is necessary that we examine our conscience to make sure we are truly prepared to receive Jesus.

CATECHISM OF THE CATHOLIC CHURCH

"It is in keeping with the very meaning of the Eucharist that the faithful, if they have the required dispositions, *receive communion when* they participate in the Mass ..."

— *CCC*, No. 1388

What are the "required dispositions" of which the *Catechism of the Catholic Church* speaks? They include:

1. That we are in a "state of grace," not conscious of any unconfessed grave sin. (If you are conscious of grave sin, you should arrange to celebrate the Sacrament of Reconciliation as soon as possible. If it is a serious situation such as not being married in the Church, you should make an appointment with the pastor of your church and discuss this with him.)

2. That we have observed the one-hour fast from food and drink (except for water and medicine) before receiving Holy Communion. Those who are advanced in age or are infirm, as well as those who care for them, are exempt from this fast.

PROCESSING TO THE ALTAR

We have witnessed two processions to the altar so far in the Mass: the first when the priests and ministers entered the church at the beginning of Mass, and the second when some members of the congregation presented the gifts of our financial offerings, the bread, and the wine to the priest. Now we leave our place and process toward the altar ourselves (if we are not in the state of mortal sin) to receive our Lord.

This procession should be dignified and reserved. In the same manner as the priest and ministers who solemnly processed at the beginning of Mass, we, too, should walk with our hands folded, contemplating the great moment that is about to take place. A message often posted on the wall of the sacristy (the place where the priest prepares for Mass) is "Celebrate this Mass as though it were your first." A similar message should be in our minds: Receive Jesus in this Communion with the same devotion and seriousness that accompanied your First Holy Communion.

It is important to remember as we approach the altar that we *receive* Jesus. We do not grab or take Communion. It is offered to us by the priest or Eucharistic minister.

In his encyclical on the Eucharist, *Ecclesia de Eucharistia*, Pope John Paul II noted that, in Communion, not only do we receive the Lord "but also that *Christ receives each of us*. He enters into friendship with us: 'You are my friends' (Jn 15:14). Indeed, it is because of him that we have life: 'He who eats me will live because of me' (Jn 6:57). Eucharistic communion brings about in a sublime way the mutual 'abiding' of Christ and each of his followers: 'Abide in me, and I in you' (Jn 15:4)" (*Ecclesia de Eucharistia*, No. 22).

Before you receive Communion, you should bow as a sign of reverence toward the Eucharistic Lord, humbling yourself before receiving Him who receives you.

RECEIVING THE EUCHARIST

There are two ways in which we may receive the Blessed Sacrament: on the tongue, or in the hand where this is permitted.

(This is allowed in the United States, but not in all countries of the world.)

The priest or Eucharistic minister will slightly raise the Blessed Sacrament as we approach, and say, "The Body of Christ."

We reply with "Amen." This is our assent to the following:

1. We believe that Jesus Christ is fully present under the appearance of this bread that we receive.

2. We believe that all His Body, the Church, teaches is true.

3. We declare that we are members of His Body, the Church.

We should receive the Lord reverently in whichever manner we choose. If on the tongue, open your mouth and extend your tongue in a reverential way, allowing the Sacrament to be placed there before closing your mouth.

If we receive the Lord in our hand, we should hold our hand open, making a throne for the Sacrament to be placed in. Again, we meaningfully take the Sacrament from our hand and place it in our mouth. We consume the Eucharist immediately.

THE FAITH OF THE EARLY CHURCH

"In approaching, therefore, do not come up with your wrists apart or with your fingers spread, but make of your left hand a throne for the right, since you are about to receive into it a King. And having hallowed your palm, receive the Body of Christ, saying over it the amen. Then, after cautiously sanctifying your eyes by the touch of the Holy Body, partake, being careful lest you lose anything of it. For whatever you might lose is clearly a loss to you from one of your own members. Tell me: if someone gave you some grains of gold, would you not hold them with all carefulness, lest you might lose something of them and thereby suffer a loss? Will you not, therefore, be much more careful in keeping watch over what is more precious than gold and gems, so that not a particle of it may escape you?"

— Saint Cyril of Jerusalem, A.D. 350

If we receive from the cup, we bow and allow the minister of the cup to present the cup to us. One should never grab the cup from the minister's hands. We drink a little and then hand the cup back to the minister.

Everything should be done reverently. After receiving the Eucharist, we walk back to our place in the congregation in the same reverential manner that we approached the altar.

CONTEMPLATING THE FRUITS OF HOLY COMMUNION

We should join in the singing, if there is any, to show again our unity as a Church. But we should also spend time contemplating this great gift that we have received. The *Catechism of the Catholic Church* lists the "fruits" of Holy Communion:

- Holy Communion unites us to the Lord. (See No. 1391)
- Holy Communion nourishes our spiritual life and gives us what we need to grow spiritually. (See No. 1392)
- Holy Communion cleanses us from past sins. (See No. 1393)
- Holy Communion strengthens the bonds of Christian love within us. (See No. 1394)
- Holy Communion makes it harder to fall into mortal sin in the future. (See No. 1395)
- Holy Communion creates the Church; through it our Lord unites us into one Body. (See No. 1396)
- Holy Communion compels us to recognize the same Lord in the poor. (See No. 1397)
- Holy Communion makes us painfully aware of the divisions that exist in the Body of Christ and bids us to pray "that all may be one." (See No. 1398)

We should use this time of intimate communion with our Lord to reflect upon the fruits of this Communion and to give thanks to the Lord for having joined Himself to us. If there is a hymn of thanksgiving sung in our church, we should raise our voices joyfully!

PRAYER AFTER COMMUNION

The Communion Rite ends with a prayer said by the priest. He invites us to pray. Everyone stands and there is a brief moment of silence as we direct our hearts to the prayer that he will say in our name. The prayer gives thanks to God for the Eucharist we have received.

If we have been attentive and have been thankful ourselves after Communion, we will find that this prayer expresses our sentiments. If, on the other hand, we have been preoccupied with other things, this prayer should help us to refocus on what is truly important at this moment.

We answer this prayer with "Amen," making it our own.

MEDITATION

When he was at table with them, he took the bread and blessed, and broke it, and gave it to them. And their eyes were opened and they recognized him; and he vanished out of their sight. They said to each other, "Did not our hearts burn within us while he talked to us on the road, while he opened to us the scriptures?"

— Luke 24: 30-32

"And their eyes were opened ..."

When our Lord gave the disciples on the road to Emmaus the bread that He had blessed and broken, "he vanished out of their sight" (Luke 24:31). It was then that they recognized Him. We receive the Lord as they did in receiving the Eucharist. Now, at the moment that He is within us, we too should reflect, as they did, on the Scriptures that He has opened to us during this Mass, especially on what has made our "hearts burn."

In our consumer-minded society, we can miss the treasure that we receive if we treat it like one more thing to "get" and then go on to the next thing. Our Lord is not a "thing." He is God, who has deigned to come intimately into our lives. We should reflect on His Presence within us and ask what He would have us do.

We should commune with our Lord and meditate on His Presence within us. We should thank Him for the great gift He has given us. We should pour our hearts out to Him and ask Him to fill us with the graces necessary to fulfill God's will for us in this life.

The same Jesus who was born in Bethlehem, preached and healed throughout Israel, who suffered and died on the cross, then rose from the dead and ascended into heaven, now is within us. We will never exhaust the multitude of wonder that should fill our hearts at this moment!

OPPORTUNITY FOR SPIRITUAL GROWTH

Continue to sing the Communion song and give great praise and thanks to God for the gift of His Son in this Eucharist. In the moment of silence that follows, pour out your heart to Jesus. Thank Him, praise Him, tell Him you love Him.

22

How to Receive the Final Blessing

CONTENTS OF THIS CHAPTER

- **Concluding Rites**
- **Final Blessing**
- **Sent Forth in Peace**

CONCLUDING RITES

After Communion, the concluding rites of the Mass bring everything to the point of sending us forth. If there are announcements to be made, they are made at this time. If there is any other parish business to be taken care of, it usually will happen at this time, too.

THE FAITH OF THE EARLY CHURCH

"And let the deacon say: Bow down to God through His Christ, and receive the blessing ...

"... And the deacon shall say, 'Depart in peace.' "

— *Apostolic Constitutions,*
A.D. 400

FINAL BLESSING

From the moment we entered the church to attend Mass, we have blessed ourselves: coming into the church; as we genuflected or bowed toward the sanctuary; at the beginning of the Mass; and over our forehead, lips, and heart before the Gospel. Now we receive a blessing.

Sometimes this blessing happens right after the priest greets us, asking the Lord's Presence to be with us. Other times there are additional prayers, and we might be told by the deacon or priest to bow our heads. In either case we should bow our heads as we trace the sign of the cross while the priest asks God to bestow His blessing upon us.

SENT FORTH IN PEACE

The wording may be lost on us, but in a very pragmatic fashion the priest or deacon is letting us know that our gathering for the Eucharistic celebration is concluding. Yet really there is more being communicated here. The Lord has come into our lives, and in the same way that the Lord sent out His disciples, He is sending us out, too.

The Mass receives its name from the concluding statement of the priest or deacon: *Ite missa est*, a Latin phrase that literally means "Go, you are dismissed," or "Go, you are sent." The fact that the Mass takes its name from this final act of the celebration points to the purpose of it. We are being sent forth on a mission.

Our Lord does not send us out into the world as orphans, but equips us for the journey. He has formed us by teaching us through His Word, which we have heard proclaimed, and He has fed us with His very Presence for our missionary activity.

All of the English options that end the Mass emphasize that we are being sent in peace. If we have given the Lord all that troubled us when we entered the doors of the church, we will find that we truly do leave with His peace. It is not an empty phrase, for the Lord is truly our only hope for peace in this world.

HOW TO RECEIVE A BLESSING

- **Bow your head slightly in a posture of receptivity.**

- **Listen to the prayer that is being prayed over you.**

- **Make the sign of the cross slowly, reverently, and deliberately.**

OPPORTUNITY FOR SPIRITUAL GROWTH

 Some churches are notorious for having huge numbers of people leave right after Communion. The reasons they leave are as numerous as there are people who do it. Here is an opportunity to grow spiritually.

- Don't judge them.
- Don't join them.
- Pray for any special needs they might have, asking Jesus to bless them as they are leaving without the final blessing.
- Ask God for the virtue of patience.

Too often we are in a hurry. Allow your faith in God and His Providence to let you sit patiently as the Mass comes to an end and you are sent forth.

23

—— How to Leave the Church ——
and Evangelize

CONTENTS OF THIS CHAPTER

- **The Closing Procession**
- **Exiting From Your Seat or Pew**
- **Encountering the Usher and Celebrant**
- **The World**
- **Meditation — "And they rose that same hour ..."**

THE CLOSING PROCESSION

At the end of the Mass the priest will go to the altar again and kiss it. After this he is joined by the other ministers in front of the altar, and after a brief moment they all bow toward the altar. While this is happening the congregation sings the final hymn that usually gives expression to the fact that we, who are now renewed, are being sent back into the world.

The ministers of the liturgy, minus the Book of the Gospels, now exit the church. The congregation should remain in their places until the end of the closing hymn.

EXITING FROM YOUR SEAT OR PEW

As you leave your pew or seat, you should face the altar and either bow or genuflect (again repeating the same action that you performed when you entered), while making the sign of the cross. Making your way to the rear of the church, you should proceed quietly. You may notice that some people remain to pray, and they should be afforded the opportunity to do so in silence.

Bless yourself again upon leaving the church, mindful that you are protecting yourself from evil and claiming your baptism. The symbolism of doing so upon leaving the church is obviously different from doing so when you enter, but it is a reminder of the missionary call of all the baptized to go out and make disciples of all people!

ENCOUNTERING THE USHER AND CELEBRANT

In most churches an usher will hand out church bulletins in the back after the Mass. Treat this person with respect. Make sure you take a bulletin, so that you can keep abreast of what is going on in the parish community. Many parishes offer excellent programs in which you can expand your knowledge of your faith.

The priest celebrant of the Mass may also be at the door. If he is, introduce yourself to him. Make yourself known in your parish.

THE WORLD

Finally, as you step outside again, you find yourself back in "your" world, with all of its difficulties and challenges. For some, walking out of the church doors means walking out into a busy street; for others it means a stroll through a green lawn to a parking lot. Sometimes leaving from a parking lot can be a great test of your faith in the Body of Christ. It has been known to happen that some are in such a rush to spread the good news they have just heard that they are not always mindful of the others who are about to set out to do the same thing. Whatever your experience is, be mindful of Jesus' Presence within you. Just as our Lord walked the streets of Jerusalem, so now He walks with you in whatever part of the world you find yourself.

Keep our Lord's Presence in mind. Bring Him with you to all areas of your life. Mention Him to your friends and co-workers. Share your faith with others. When you are embarrassed or fearful of doing so, invoke the Holy Spirit's help.

The great gift that you have received is not for you alone, but for all people. Do your part to bring the faith to them. This is what you are "sent" for at the end of Mass. Do not fail to fulfill your mission!

MEDITATION

"And they rose that same hour and returned to Jerusalem; and they found the eleven gathered together and those who were with them, who said, "The Lord has risen indeed, and has appeared to Simon!" Then they told what had happened on the road, and how he was known to them in the breaking of the bread. As they were saying this, Jesus himself stood among them, and said to them, 'Peace to you.' "

— Luke 24:33-36

"And they rose that same hour ..."

When Jesus first met the disciples walking on the road to Emmaus they were sad. The journey seemed to take the entire day, so that when they reached their destination it was already evening. But notice what happens to them once they encounter the Lord in the "breaking of the bread." The Gospel of Luke tells us that "they rose that same hour and returned to Jerusalem"

OPPORTUNITIES FOR SPIRITUAL GROWTH

Much has happened during this Mass; now what will you do with the Scripture Readings that you have heard?

What will you do with the Lord's Presence that you now carry within you?

Use every opportunity to share the "good news" with your family and with others you come into contact with throughout the day. Witness all that you have seen and heard.

(Luke 24:33). They could not contain their joy and quickly made it back to Jerusalem!

So it should be with us. If we apply ourselves fully, unafraid of sharing with our Lord all that bothers us when we enter the church, listening to what He says to us in the Scriptures, allowing Him to feed our hunger — then we, too, should leave every Mass with a joy that cannot be contained. We should find ourselves eager to share the good news of what a difference life makes when we are in a relationship with Jesus Christ.

We will find that like the disciples, our missionary efforts will be rewarded by the very Presence of our Lord in our lives and He will truly bless us!

Appendix I

Prayers Before Mass

CONTENTS OF THIS CHAPTER

- **Prayer of Saint Ambrose**
- **Prayer of Saint Thomas Aquinas**
- **Prayer to the Blessed Virgin Mary**
- **Prayer to Saint Joseph**
- **Prayer to All Angels and Saints**

The following are prayers that have been traditionally presented as excellent aids in preparing oneself for the celebration of the Mass. You might find it helpful to pray a few of these even before you leave home for Mass.

PRAYER OF SAINT AMBROSE

Lord Jesus Christ, I approach Thy banquet table in fear and trembling, for I am a sinner, and dare not rely on my own worth, but only on Thy goodness and mercy. I am defiled by my many sins in body and soul, and by my unguarded thoughts and words. Gracious God of majesty and awe, I seek Thy protection, I look for Thy healing. Poor troubled sinner that I am, I appeal to Thee, the fountain of all mercy. I cannot bear Thy judgment, but I trust in Thy salvation. Lord, I show my wounds to Thee and uncover my shame before Thee. I know my sins are many and great, and they fill me with fear, but I hope in Thy mercies, for they cannot be numbered.

Lord Jesus Christ, Eternal King, God and man, crucified for mankind, look upon me with mercy and hear my prayer, for I trust in Thee. Have mercy on me, full of sorrow and sin, for the depth of Thy compassion never ends.

Praise to Thy saving sacrifice, offered on the wood of the cross for me and for all mankind. Praise to the noble and precious blood, flowing from the wounds of my crucified Lord Jesus Christ and washing away the sins of the whole world.

Remember, Lord, Thy creature, whom Thou hast redeemed with Thy blood; I repent my sins, and I long to put right what I have done. Merciful Father, take away all my offenses and sins; purify me in body and soul, and make me worthy to taste the Holy of Holies. May Thy body and blood, which I intend to receive, although I am unworthy, be for me the remission of my sins, the washing away of my guilt, the end of my evil thoughts, and the rebirth of my better instincts. May it incite me to do the works pleasing to Thee and profitable to my health in body and soul, and be a firm defense against the wiles of my enemies. Amen.

PRAYER OF SAINT THOMAS AQUINAS

Almighty and ever-lasting God, I approach the sacrament of Thy only-begotten Son, our Lord Jesus Christ. I come sick to the doctor of life, unclean to the fountain of mercy, blind to the radiance of eternal light, and poor and needy to the Lord of heaven and earth. Therefore, I implore Thee in Thy great generosity, to heal my sickness, to wash away my defilement, to enlighten my blindness, to enrich my poverty, and to clothe my nakedness, so that I may receive the bread of angels, the King of kings, and the Lord of lords with reverence and humility, with contrition and devotion, with purity and faith, and with such purpose and determination that will be expedient to the salvation of my soul. Grant me, I beseech Thee, that I may not only receive the Sacrament of the Body and Blood of the Lord, but also the reality and power of the Sacrament. O most kind God, grant that I may receive the Body of Thine only-begotten Son, our Lord Jesus Christ, born of the Virgin Mary, and so received that I may be worthy to be incorporated into His mystical body, and numbered among His members. O most loving Father, grant me Thy beloved Son, which I now receive under the veil of a sacrament, that I may one day behold Him face to face in glory, Who lives and reigns with Thee in the unity of the Holy Spirit, God, forever. Amen.

PRAYER TO THE BLESSED VIRGIN MARY

Mother of mercy and of love, most blessed Virgin Mary, I, a poor and unworthy sinner, fly to you with all my heart and all my affection. I implore your loving kindness, that even as you did stand beside your dearly beloved Son as He hung upon the cross, so please also stand by me, a poor sinner, and by the priest who is offering Mass here today and beside all thy faithful people receiving the most sacred Body of thy Son. Grant us, that by thy grace, we may offer a worthy and acceptable sacrifice in the sight of the most high and undivided Trinity and receive it worthily and fruitfully. Amen.

PRAYER TO SAINT JOSEPH

O Blessed Joseph, happy man, to whom it was given not only to see and to hear that God Whom many kings longed to see, and saw not, to hear, and heard not; but also to carry Him in your arms, to embrace Him, to clothe Him, and guard and defend Him.

V. Pray for us, O Blessed Joseph.
R. That we may be made worthy of the promises of Christ.

O God, Who has given us a royal priesthood, we beseech Thee, that as Blessed Joseph was found worthy to touch with his hands, and to bear in his arms, Thy only-begotten Son, born of the Virgin Mary, so may we be made fit, by cleanness of heart and blamelessness of life, to minister at Thy holy altar; may we, this day, with reverent devotion partake of the Sacred Body and Blood of Your only begotten Son, and may we in the world to come be accounted worthy of receiving an ever-lasting reward. Through the same Christ our Lord. Amen.

PRAYER TO ALL ANGELS AND SAINTS

Angels, Archangels, Thrones, Dominations, Principalities, Powers, heavenly Virtues, Cherubim and Seraphim; all Saints of God, holy men and women, and for you especially my patrons: deign to intercede for me that I may be worthy to offer this Sacrifice to almighty God, to the praise and glory of His name, for my own welfare and also that of all His holy Church. Amen.

Appendix II

Prayers After Mass

CONTENTS OF THIS CHAPTER

- **Prayers of Saint Ignatius of Loyola**
  - *Anima Christi*
  - **Prayer of Self-Dedication to Jesus Christ (*Suscipe*)**
- **Prayer Before a Crucifix**
- **Prayer of Saint Thomas Aquinas**
- **Prayer of Saint Bonaventure**
- **Universal Prayer of Pope Clement XI**
- **Prayer to the Blessed Virgin Mary**
- **Prayer to Saint Joseph**
- **Prayer in Honor of the Day's Saint**

The following are prayers that you can pray in thanksgiving after Mass.

PRAYERS OF SAINT IGNATIUS OF LOYOLA

Anima Christi

> Soul of Christ, sanctify me.
> Body of Christ, save me.
> Blood of Christ, inebriate me.
> Water from the side of Christ, wash me.
> Passion of Christ, strengthen me.
> O good Jesus, hear me.
> Within Thy wounds, hide me.
> Separated from Thee let me never be.
> From the malignant enemy, defend me.
> At the hour of death, call me.
> To come to Thee, bid me,
> That I may praise Thee in the company
> Of Thy Saints, for all eternity. Amen.

Prayer of Self-Dedication to Jesus Christ *(Suscipe)*

Lord Jesus Christ, take all my freedom, my memory, my understanding, and my will. All that I have and cherish Thou hast given me. I surrender it all to be guided by Thy will. Thy grace and Thy love are wealth enough for me. Give me these, Lord Jesus, and I ask for nothing more. Amen.

PRAYER BEFORE A CRUCIFIX

Behold, O good and most sweet Jesus, I fall upon my knees before Thee, and with most fervent desire beg and beseech Thee that Thou wouldst impress upon my heart a lively sense of faith, hope and charity, true repentance for my sins, and a firm resolve to make amends. And with deep affection and grief, I reflect upon

Thy five wounds, having before my eyes that which Thy prophet David spoke about Thee, O good Jesus: "They have pierced my hands and feet, they have counted all my bones." Amen.

PRAYER OF SAINT THOMAS AQUINAS

Lord, Father all-powerful, and ever-living God, I thank Thee, for even though I am a sinner, Thy unprofitable servant, not because of my worth, but in the kindness of Thy mercy, Thou hast fed me with the precious Body and Blood of Thy Son, our Lord Jesus Christ. I pray that this holy communion may not bring me condemnation and punishment but forgiveness and salvation. May it be a helmet of faith and a shield of good will. May it purify me from evil ways and put an end to my evil passions. May it bring me charity and patience, humility and obedience, and growth in power to do good. May it be my strong defense against all my enemies, visible and invisible, and the perfect calming of all my evil impulses, bodily and spiritual. May it unite me more closely to Thee, the one true God, and lead me safely through death to everlasting happiness with Thee. And I pray that Thou willest lead me, a sinner, to the banquet where Thou with Thy Son and Holy Spirit, art true and perfect light, total fulfillment, everlasting joy, gladness without end, and perfect happiness to Thy saints. Grant this through Christ our Lord. Amen.

PRAYER OF SAINT BONAVENTURE

Pierce, O most Sweet Lord Jesus, my inmost soul with the most joyous and healthful wound of Thy love, with true, serene, and most holy apostolic charity, that my soul may ever languish and melt with love and longing for Thee, that it may yearn for Thee and faint for Thy courts, and long to be dissolved and to be with Thee.

Grant that my soul may hunger after Thee, the bread of angels, the refreshment of holy souls, our daily and supersubstantial bread, having all sweetness and savor and every delight of taste; let my heart ever hunger after and feed upon Thee, upon whom the angels desire to look, and may my inmost soul be filled with the sweetness of Thy savor; may it ever thirst after Thee, the fountain of life, the fountain of wisdom and knowledge, the fountain of eternal light, the torrent of pleasure, the richness of the house of God.

May it ever compass Thee, seek Thee, find Thee, run to Thee, attain Thee, meditate upon Thee, speak of Thee, and do all things to the praise and glory of Thy name, with humility and discretion, with love and delight, with ease and affection, and with perseverance unto the end; may Thou alone be ever my hope, my entire assurance, my riches, my delight, my pleasure, my joy, my rest and tranquility, my peace, my sweetness, my fragrance, my sweet savor, my food, my refreshment, my refuge, my help, my wisdom, my portion, my possession and my treasure, in whom may my mind and my heart be fixed and firmly rooted immovably henceforth and for ever. Amen.

UNIVERSAL PRAYER OF POPE CLEMENT XI

Lord, I believe in you: increase my faith.
I trust in you: strengthen my trust.
I love you: let me love you more and more.
I am sorry for my sins: deepen my sorrow.
I worship you as my first beginning,
I long for you as my last end.
I praise you as my constant helper,
and call on you as my loving protector.
Guide me by your wisdom,
correct me with your justice,

comfort me with your mercy,
protect me with your power.
I offer you, Lord, my thoughts: to be fixed on you;
my words: to have you for their theme;
my actions: to reflect my love for you;
my sufferings: to be endured for your greater glory.
I want to do what you ask of me: in the way you ask,
for as long as you ask, because you ask it.
Lord, enlighten my understanding, strengthen my will,
purify my heart, and make me holy.
Help me to repent of my past sins
and to resist temptation in the future.
Help me to rise above my human weaknesses
and to grow stronger as a Christian.
Let me love you, my Lord and my God,
and see myself as I really am:
a pilgrim in this world,
a Christian
called to respect and love all whose lives I touch,
those in authority over me
or those under my authority,
my friends and my enemies.
Help me to conquer anger with gentleness,
greed by generosity, apathy by fervor.
Help me to forget myself and reach out toward others.
Make me prudent in planning, courageous in taking risks.
Make me patient in suffering, unassuming in prosperity.
Keep me, Lord, attentive in prayer,
temperate in food and drink,
diligent in my work, firm in my good intentions.
Let my conscience be clear, my conduct without fault,
my speech blameless, my life well-ordered.

Put me on guard against my human weaknesses.
Let me cherish your love for me, keep your law,
and come at last to your salvation.
Teach me to realize that this world is passing,
that my true future is the happiness of heaven,
that life on earth is short,
and the life to come eternal.
Help me to prepare for death
with a proper fear of judgment,
but a greater trust in your goodness.
Lead me safely through death to the endless joy of heaven.
Grant this through Christ our Lord. Amen.

PRAYER TO THE BLESSED VIRGIN MARY

O Mary, most holy Virgin and Mother, behold, I have received thy most beloved Son, Jesus Christ, whom thou conceivedst in thy spotless womb, bore, nursed, and held with thy sweet embraces. Behold Him at whose sight thou willst rejoice and be filled with every delight. With love I humbly return Him and offer Him to thee, to hold once more, to love with all thy heart, and to offer to the Holy Trinity as our supreme act of worship for thy honor and glory and for my good and the good of all the world. Therefore I ask thee, most loving Mother, to ask God for forgiveness of all my sins, abundant graces to help me serve Him more faithfully, and for that final grace that I may praise Him with thee for ever and ever. Amen.

PRAYER TO SAINT JOSEPH

Guardian of virgins and father, Saint Joseph, to whose faithful custody Innocence itself, Christ Jesus, and Mary, Virgin of virgins, was committed; I pray and beseech thee by each of these dear pledges, Jesus and Mary, that, being preserved from all uncleanness, I may with spotless mind, pure heart, and a chaste body, ever serve Jesus and Mary most chastely all the days of my life. Amen.

PRAYER IN HONOR OF THE DAY'S SAINT

O Saint N., in whose honor I have offered the bloodless sacrifice of the Body and Blood of Christ, grant by thy powerful intercession with God, that, by the utility of this mystery, I may obtain the merits of the passion and death of this same Christ our Savior. And with its frequency come to salvation. Amen.

Appendix III

———— Study Guide ————

The following review and reflection questions are provided for each section of the book. When used in a study group, a session might begin by reading the Scripture and meditation found in the book for that section (where applicable) and then actually reading aloud the parts of the Mass being studied. Then go over the review questions from the section, followed by the reflection questions. Participants should read the section to be studied before it is discussed in the group.

In this guide, I have added references to two books that I have written since *The How-To Book of the Mass* was originally written that in some cases give a fuller treatment which a group or individual might find helpful. One of these is a Lenten meditation book entitled *The Power of the Cross: Applying the Passion of Christ to Your Life*, published by Our Sunday Visitor (2004). The other is a follow-up book to this one on the Mass entitled *How to Get the Most Out of the Eucharist*, also published by Our Sunday Visitor (2005).

WHAT *IS* THE MASS? (Pages 25-28)

Review Questions
1. Where does the word "Mass" come from?
2. Who are the two groups dismissed from the Mass at different times?
3. What is "the liturgy"?
4. Can you give at least three other names used for the Mass?
5. How does the *Catechism of the Catholic Church* define the Mass?

Reflection Questions
1. Read Matthew 28:18-20. How is Jesus' command for His disciples to "go" expressed in the central act of Catholic worship?
2. Read Acts 2:44-47, a description of the earliest Church. What does the breaking of the bread refer to and how is that experienced in the Church today?
3. Pope John Paul II writes in *Mane Nobiscum Domine*, his apostolic letter on the Year of the Eucharist, that "the dismissal at the end of each Mass is *a charge* given to Christians, inviting them to work for the spread of the gospel and the imbuing of society with Christian values" (No. 24). How might you focus more on the mission that Christ is giving you (at every Mass) to evangelize?

See Also ...
How to Get the Most Out of the Eucharist (Pages 116-120 for a fuller treatment on the "Go" of Jesus)
The Power of the Cross ("Day 1: The Cross of Christ Teaches Us Our Mission")

HOW TO GET SOMETHING OUT OF MASS (Pages 29-36)

Review Questions

1. What areas of our life might we be keeping off-limits to Jesus in our prayer?
2. What are the three opportunities for spiritual growth mentioned in this section?
3. Why were people in the Gospels scandalized by Jesus?

Reflection Questions

1. Is there an area of your life that you tend to block the Son of God from entering?
2. Is there a person you know who needs help to return to Christ's Church? (If this is done in a group study, everyone should pray for those who need God's help.)

See Also ...

How to Get the Most Out of the Eucharist (Pages 38-40 on adoring God above anything else)

The Power of the Cross ("Day 15: The Cross of Christ Transforms How We Worship")

1. HOW TO ENTER THE CHURCH (Pages 37-47)

Meditation (Page 46)

Review Questions

1. What do church doors symbolize?
2. Why do Catholics bless themselves with holy water?
3. Where do the words for the sign of the cross come from?
4. Where does this water come from and what makes it holy?
5. What does Jesus save us from?
6. When is it correct to genuflect? To bow?
7. What does the tabernacle contain?
8. What does a lit sanctuary lamp signify? Unlit?

9. Give three things the altar symbolizes in a Catholic Church.
10. What is a catechumen?

Reflection Questions
1. Read Genesis 3 and the *Catechism* entry found on Page 41. Discuss what the kingdom of God is like versus the fallen world of original sin.
2. What can you learn from the acts of dipping your hand into the waters of baptism, making the sign of the cross, and invoking the Triune God as you enter a church? Reflect on what each of these three acts symbolizes and what they might mean for you personally.
3. Why do you think a catechumen would be dismissed before the recitation of the creed? What does this say about those who are baptized and remain?
4. When the book says, "This water is the price of your admission (Page 42)," what might the author mean?
5. What is the entrance of your parish church like? What symbols are there?

See Also …
How to Get the Most Out of the Eucharist (Pages 24-26, "What Jesus Has Saved us From"; Pages 58-59, "Teach Me to Pray!")
The Power of the Cross ("Day 3: The Cross of Christ Teaches Us How to Pray")

2. HOW TO CELEBRATE THE OPENING RITES (Pages 49-57)

Meditation (Page 56)

Review Questions
1. What is the purpose of the opening hymn?

2. Who celebrates the Mass?
3. What is a reader? server? deacon? celebrant?
4. What is the purpose of making the sign of the cross?
5. Where do the greetings used by the celebrant come from?
6. Where do our responses come from?
7. Who was Saint Paul?

Reflection Questions
1. According to the author, the opening hymn can also serve as a way for each of us individually to "die to ourselves." How do you react when the opening hymn is not one of your favorites?
2. The greetings at Mass place us back in the time of Jesus, reflecting common greetings used in His time that are found in Scripture. How can knowing this help us to enter more fully in the ritual we are a part of?
3. Everyone has a role to fulfill in the Mass. Discuss how each role, when fulfilled in a faith-filled way, enhances the celebration of the Mass.

See Also ...
How to Get the Most Out of the Eucharist (Pages 66-69, "The Body of Christ")
The Power of the Cross ("Ash Wednesday: Eternal Life or Death?")

3. HOW TO CELEBRATE THE PENITENTIAL RITE (Pages 59-68)

Meditation (Page 67)

Review Questions
1. What practice does the *Didache* (quoted at the beginning of the chapter) hold out as "the way of life"?
2. Why is it important to be silent in prayer?

3. Where does the practice of "striking one's breast" come from?

4. Why do some Catholics still strike their breast at different times in the liturgy? When should we be doing this?

5. Does the prayer of absolution said during the Penitential Rite absolve us of serious sin?

6. How did the ancient Israelites use the word "Lord"?

7. What language is *Kyrie*?

8. Where does the phrase "Lord, have mercy" come from?

Reflection Questions

1. Read Luke 18:9-14, the parable of the Pharisee and tax collector at prayer. What does this parable teach us about how a follower of Christ ought to pray? How is this exemplified in the Church's supreme prayer, the Mass?

2. Read the Confiteor out loud and slowly. Whom do we confess to in this prayer? Whom do we ask to pray for us to God? How seriously do you take the request offered by those in church with you to pray for them?

3. How can the gestures used during the Mass serve as an aid in meditating on the Bible?

See Also ...

How to Get the Most Out of the Eucharist (Pages 56-58, "We Are All Sinners"; Pages 67-69, "How Do We Respond?")

The Power of the Cross ("Day 6: The Cross of Christ Teaches Us Reconciliation" and "Day 14: The Cross of Christ Unites God's Mercy and Love")

4. HOW TO SING THE GLORIA (Pages 69-78)

Meditation (Page 75)

Review Questions

1. Where does the prayer the Gloria come from?

2. When is the Gloria not said at Mass and why?
3. What is a doxology?
4. What does "glory" mean in the Scriptures?
5. What can we learn from the message of the angels in Luke's Gospel and where Jesus is to be found today?
6. What is Advent?
7. What is Lent?
8. When was the Gloria prayed in the early Church?

Reflection Questions
1. Pray the Gloria and think about what the chapter says are the three distinct sections of it. How can you take the experiences of your life and make them part of this prayer?
2. What lessons can we learn, beyond what the book mentions, when the Gloria is omitted at Mass?
3. Praying a doxology is an ancient way to end a prayer, something that is still practiced in the Church's daily prayer, the Liturgy of the Hours, when a "Glory Be" is prayed at the end of Psalms and Canticles. How can you apply the practice of giving God praise throughout your day?

See Also ...
How to Get the Most Out of the Eucharist (Page 42, "Living in Thanksgiving")
The Power of the Cross ("Day 5: The Cross of Christ Teaches How to Trust and Give Thanks")

5. HOW TO SAY AMEN TO THE OPENING PRAYER (Pages 79-83)

Review Questions
1. What does it mean to pray?
2. Why is the opening prayer called "the collect"?
3. Why does the priest say this prayer?

4. What are the four parts of his prayer?
5. What is the meaning of the word "amen"?

Reflection Questions
1. Read Luke 11:9-10 (quoted on Page 80). How often do you do what Jesus tells His disciples?
2. How can one use the silent period to more fully enter into the prayer?
3. How might the different meanings of the word "amen" change the way you view what you say when you speak this word in the future?

See Also ...
    How to Get the Most Out of the Eucharist (Page 30, "Help From the Fathers of the Church")
    The Power of the Cross ("Day 26: The Cross of Christ Illumines Our Choices")

6. HOW TO UNDERSTAND THE LITURGY OF THE WORD (Pages 85-92)

Meditation (Page 91)

Review Questions
1. What are the two parts of the Mass? Who is allowed in the church for each part?
2. What was the Covenant at Mount Sinai like? How is the New Covenant of Jesus similar?
3. How is the recitation of the creed like the assent given by the Israelites in the desert to the Mount Sinai Covenant?
4. How does the saying of the crowd "His blood be on us and our children!" best understood in terms of the ratification of the New Covenant by the people?
5. What is an ambo? Where is it located in your church?

6. What does "Word" mean when referred to as the "Word of God"?
7. Where do the readings read at Mass come from?

Reflection Questions
1. Catechumens are dismissed at the conclusion of the Liturgy of the Word. Why? How does this affect you as a baptized Catholic or catechumen?
2. This chapter made a lot out of understanding the New Testament by knowing the Old Testament. Can you think of some other New Testament teachings that only make sense when we have a better knowledge of the entire Bible?

See Also ...
How to Get the Most Out of the Eucharist (Pages 75-82, "Incline Your Ear to the Lord")
The Power of the Cross ("Day 11: The Cross of Christ Unites in Liberty")

7. HOW TO LISTEN TO THE FIRST READING (Pages 93-100)

Review Questions
1. What is a Lectionary?
2. Why are the Bible readings altered slightly when read at Mass?
3. What translation of Scripture is used at Masses in English in the United States?
4. What part of the Bible is the First Reading from outside of the Easter Season? What book of the Bible is read for the First Reading during the Easter Season?
5. What is another name for the Old and New Testaments?
6. Why does the Catholic Old Testament contain more books than the non-Catholic one?

7. When the First Reading is from the Old Testament, what other reading at Mass is it connected with?
8. What book of the Bible is read as the First Reading during the Easter Season?
9. How is what is said by the reader at the conclusion of the First Reading similar to what is said when we approach to receive Holy Communion?
10. How does Saint Paul use the words "Thanks be to God" in his letters?

Reflection Questions
1. The book gives an example from the First Sunday of Lent (Page 96) on a connection between the First Reading and the Gospel. Can you find a connection either with last Sunday's readings or this Sunday's?
2. What lesson can be gained by hearing the Acts of the Apostles during the Easter Season as it applies to us who have been baptized in Christ?
3. Think of how listening to the Word of God at Mass enables you to enter into a covenant with God. What does the Word of God require of you in order to enter more fully into this covenant?

See Also …

To better understand what a Lectionary is, you might ask your local parish to let you look at a Lectionary to see how it arranges the readings used at Mass. Bring a Bible with you and compare how the readings appear in the Lectionary with how the same text appears in your Bible.

How to Get the Most Out of the Eucharist (Page 85, "3. Fostering an Attitude of Mindfulness" and "5. A Prayer for Today")

The Power of the Cross ("Day 13: The Cross of Christ Unites
Us in the Work We Have to Do")

8. HOW TO RESPOND TO THE RESPONSORIAL PSALM
(Pages 101-107)

Review Questions
1. Where do the Psalms come from?
2. Who wrote the Psalms?
3. What does the word "psalms" mean?
4. Who first said that the Psalms had references to Jesus in them?
5. What did the early Church believe about the Psalms and Jesus?
6. What is the official prayer of the Church largely made up of the Psalms called?
7. What is the Responsorial Psalm linked to in the Liturgy of the Word?

Reflection Questions
1. Open your Bible to the Book of Psalms and choose one. Read it slowly and try to see how it might reveal the inner life of Jesus. What insights do you gain?
2. Try praying Morning or Evening Prayer of the Liturgy of the Hours. Why do you think the Psalms are deemed so important to the official prayer of the Church?

See Also ...
How to Get the Most Out of the Eucharist (Page 85, "5. A Prayer for Today")
The Power of the Cross ("Day 21: The Cross of Christ Transforms How We See Ourselves")

9. HOW TO LISTEN TO THE SECOND READING (Pages 109-113)

Review Questions

1. What part of the Bible does the Second Reading proclaimed at Mass come from?
2. How is it connected to the First Reading and Gospel?
3. What is meant by the term "continuous reading"?
4. What is the difference between a "letter" and a "Gospel"?
5. Is the Book of Revelation a letter?
6. What is the beginning of the spiritual life according to the Vatican statement quoted in this chapter?

Reflection Questions

1. Listening to a letter being read aloud gives us one side of a conversation. Read the Second Reading from either this Sunday or last Sunday, and try to ascertain what the apostle might be addressing to the community he originally wrote. Does the parish you attend suffer similar problems? What are the applications you can take from the letter with regard to your own life?
2. Locate a commentary on the letter that is currently being used as a Second Reading. What was the situation of the community that the apostle was writing to according to the commentary?

See Also ...

How to Get the Most Out of the Eucharist (Page 85, "5. A Prayer for Today")

The Power of the Cross ("Day 19: The Cross of Christ Transforms Our Lives")

10. HOW TO LISTEN TO THE GOSPEL (Pages 115-123)

Review Questions

1. What is the Book of the Gospels? What does it represent?

2. What does "Alleluia" mean?
3. When is the Alleluia not sung or said during Mass?
4. What does the word "gospel" mean?
5. Who may read the Gospel at Mass?
6. What type of preparation do we make symbolically before we listen to the Gospel?
7. What might we say as we trace the sign of the cross on our foreheads, lips, and heart?
8. What does it mean when we read that the *General Instruction of the Roman Missal* says that in the Gospel we "acknowledge and confess Christ present and speaking" to us?

Reflection Questions

1. Are there competing gospels in our culture? In other words, are others preaching another type of "good" news to us that clouds our ability to accept the message of Jesus as the real way to be delivered from our fallen state?
2. How can we prepare ourselves to better hear the Gospels, to learn in a more accurate way how Jesus has revealed God to us?

See Also ...

To better understand what a Book of the Gospels is, you might ask your local parish to let you look at their Book of the Gospels to see how it arranges the Gospel Readings used at Mass. Bring a Bible with you and compare how the readings appear in the Book of the Gospels with how the same text appears in your Bible.

How to Get the Most Out of the Eucharist (Page 24, "Do You Know What I Have Done for You?"; Page 55, "The Fallen World")

The Power of the Cross ("Saturday after Ash Wednesday: The Power of the Cross — A Matter of Life and Death")

11. HOW TO HEAR A GREAT HOMILY *EVERY TIME* YOU ATTEND MASS (Pages 125-131)

Meditation (Page 130)

Review Questions
1. What is a homily?
2. Who can preach a homily at Mass?
3. How can we pray for the preacher?
4. How can we better listen to a homily?
5. In the story of the brothers who came to Saint Antony of the Desert, what did Saint Antony diagnose as their spiritual problem?

Reflection Questions
1. What homily have you heard at Mass that has made you want to deepen your relationship with Christ? Was there anything special about it that caused the words of the preacher to have this effect upon you?
2. Try the method suggested in the book of both praying for the preacher and asking God to give you a "word" in the preacher's homily. What happens?

See Also ...
> *How to Get the Most Out of the Eucharist* (Pages 81-86, "Incline Your Ear to the Lord")
> *The Power of the Cross* ("Day 16: The Cross of Christ Transforms How We See Jesus")

12. TIME OUT! WHERE ARE *THEY* GOING AND WHO ARE THEY? (Pages 133-138)

Meditation (Page 137)

Review Questions
1. Who are catechumens and candidates for full communion? Why do they leave after the homily?

2. What should we do as the catechumens and candidates are exiting the church building?
3. How can a Catholic interested in assisting those on this faith journey help them?
4. What are the catechumens and candidates doing during the remainder of the Mass?

Reflection Questions
1. What can the time of preparation and formation taken by those in the Catechumenate teach us who were baptized as infants?
2. How might your parish help those raised in the Church to model their own spiritual formation after that of the Catechumenate?

See Also ...

You might invite the head of the Catechumenate in your parish to speak to your group about the process. Also ask someone who is currently enrolled or someone who has gone through the process to speak to your group.

How to Get the Most Out of the Eucharist (Pages 125-130, "Appendix: How to Get the Most Out of the Eucharist When You Cannot Receive Communion")
The Power of the Cross ("Day 41: Taking Up Our Cross to Stay with Jesus")

13. HOW TO PRAY THE CREED (Pages 139-148)

Meditation (Page 147)

Review Questions
1. How is the recitation of the creed similar to the proclamation of the people that "all that the Lord has said we will do," which the Israelites said in response to Moses' reading of the Covenant?

2. What is the "Credo" and what does the word mean?

3. What does it mean to believe in God? In one God? In Jesus Christ? In the Holy Spirit and the Catholic Church?

4. When should we genuflect during the recitation of the creed? When should we bow? Why do we do this?

5. What is meant by the "resurrection of the body and life everlasting"?

6. What replaces the creed on Easter Sunday?

Reflection Questions

1. How can you learn to trust God first in your life? What steps can you take to trust in the Holy Spirit and the Church?

2. What can you do to increase your understanding of the tenets of the creed you profess to believe?

3. What might you do to pass on this faith to others?

4. What parts of the creed take you "further" than where you are at right now? Can you see how faith is an important virtue in this regard?

5. When were you baptized? How has your faith matured since then?

See Also ...

How to Get the Most Out of the Eucharist (Pages 41-47, "Adore God with Praise and Thanksgiving"; Pages 51-52, "Confess Your Belief in God")

The Power of the Cross ("Day 5: The Cross of Christ Teaches Us How to Trust and Give Thanks")

14. HOW TO PRAY THE PRAYERS OF THE FAITHFUL (Pages 149-154)

Meditation (Page 153)

Review Questions

1. When we pray the Prayers of the Faithful, how do we act as Christ?
2. What do the Scripture passages quoted in the chapter reveal about Jesus' teaching on prayer?
3. What is the usual order of those prayed for in the petitions of the Prayers of the Faithful?
4. In the meditation, what is the significance of the word "constrained" in the Emmaus story?

Reflection Questions

1. How can your parish become more prayerful?
2. Reflecting on Jesus' teaching on prayer and its power, how might you enter into prayer more often?
3. Why do we have a duty to pray for the universal Church?
4. What would it be like to have faith the size of a mustard seed?

See Also ...

How to Get the Most Out of the Eucharist (Page 98, "Where Two or Three Gather Together in My Name")

The Power of the Cross ("Day 3: The Cross of Christ Teaches Us How to Pray")

15. HOW TO JOIN IN THE PREPARATION OF THE GIFTS (Pages 155-165)

Meditation (Page 164)

Review Questions

1. How are the elements of bread and wine symbolic of the congregation?
2. In the early Church, what was presented at the time of the collection? How does giving money amount to the same thing today?

3. What is a corporal? a purificator? a Sacramentary? a chalice?
4. What is the Jewish blessing known as the Kiddush?
5. What do you do when seated in the congregation and you are being incensed at Mass?
6. What does incense symbolize?
7. What does the hand washing of the priest symbolize?
8. What biblical examples are there of God rejecting a sacrifice?
9. How can you go about having a Mass said for someone or some group?
10. How can we offer our sacrifice at Mass?

Reflection Questions

1. Given the early Christians' way of offering gifts to the Church (see "What Is It?" on Page 159), how might our practice of Christian stewardship imitate theirs today?
2. Think about the service roles of those who take up the collection, who bring up the gifts, and the priest who offers the gifts for the whole body of believers. How does each contribute and, at the same time, how does each role differ?
3. What might be a modern way in which someone could offer an unacceptable sacrifice to God?
4. How can you be more mindful of offering your sacrifice at Mass?

See Also ...

How to Get the Most Out of the Eucharist (the entire book is essentially about offering your sacrifice at every Mass you attend)

The Power of the Cross ("Day 36: Taking Up Our Cross in Abandonment")

16. HOW TO GIVE THANKS TO GOD IN THE EUCHARISTIC PRAYER (Pages 167-177)

Review Questions

1. What are the key parts of the Eucharistic Prayers said at Mass?
2. Where did the "Holy, Holy, Holy" originate?
3. What does Saint Cyril of Alexandria teach about the meaning of "lifting up our hearts"?
4. What is the *Sanctus*? Where does it come from?
5. What does the word *hosanna* mean in English?
6. What does the posture of kneeling symbolize?
7. What does *epiclesis* mean?
8. When do Catholics believe that the bread and wine offered at Mass become the Body and Blood of Christ?
9. What is " transubstantiation"?
10. What is "ocular" Communion?
11. What is the *anamnesis*?
12. Why do we acclaim the great mystery of our faith right after the separate consecration of bread and wine?
13. What parts of the Eucharistic Prayer are prayed by the lay faithful in attendance at Mass?

Reflection Questions

1. The Eucharistic Prayer points toward the power of God's Word spoken by the presider. How does understanding this encourage you to reverence the Scriptures?
2. The Jewish and Christian sense of "memorial" makes an event present. How does understanding this truth change the way you experience the Eucharistic Prayer at Mass?
3. How can you enter more fully into the prayer of the presider during the Eucharistic Prayer?

See Also ...

How to Get the Most Out of the Eucharist (Pages 95-101,
"Invite the Lord to Come")

The Power of the Cross ("Day 40: Taking Up the Cross in Imitation of Christ")

17. HOW TO SAY AMEN TO THE EUCHARISTIC PRAYER (Pages 179-182)

Review Questions
1. What is a doxology?
2. Why is the "amen" said by all at the conclusion of the Eucharistic Prayer called the "Great Amen"?

Reflection Question
1. How can you make the "Great Amen" more meaningful?

See Also ...

How to Get the Most Out of the Eucharist (Page 90, "What Is
the Purpose of Fasting?")

The Power of the Cross ("Day 8: The Cross Unites the Tempo-
ral and the Eternal")

18. HOW TO PRAY THE LORD'S PRAYER (Pages 183-191)

Review Questions
1. How many times a day were the early Christians instructed to pray the Our Father in the *Didache*?
2. Why do we address God as "*our* Father" and not like Jesus did when He called God "*my* father"?
3. How many petitions are there in the Lord's Prayer?
4. Is the Our Father found in the Bible?
5. What does it mean to pray for God's kingdom to come?
6. What is meant by "our daily bread"?

7. Why do we ask to be forgiven as we forgive?

8. What is meant by "temptation" in the Our Father?

9. What is the "evil" that we ask to be delivered from?

10. What is the origin of the short prayer "for the kingdom, the power, and the glory are yours"?

Reflection Questions

1. Discuss what each aspect of the Our Father means. Read the *Catechism of the Catholic Church* (Nos. 2761-2854) or the *Compendium of the Catechism of the Catholic Church* (Nos. 578-598) for an excellent commentary on this prayer.

2. How is the Our Father a prayer for the Second Coming of Christ, and how does this make it the perfect prayer to be prayed in the context of the Mass?

See Also ...

How to Get the Most Out of the Eucharist (Page 98, "Expectation of the Lord's Coming")

The Power of the Cross ("Day 31: The Cross of Christ Restores the Image of God")

19. HOW TO GIVE THE SIGN OF PEACE (Pages 193-196)

Review Questions

1. What does being "in communion with the Lord" mean (list the three implications highlighted in the chapter)?

2. How is this highlighted by the Scripture passages quoted in the chapter?

3. In what ways can you make the sign of peace truly peaceful?

4. What should you do if you have an illness that could be spread by contact with others during the sign of peace?

Reflection Questions

1. There is a grace that is offered to us here. Peace is given to us from the Lord. How can we overcome our natural aversions and, accepting the grace of Christ, truly offer the sign of peace to those around us?

2. How should you react to someone who refuses to give you the sign of peace at Mass or appears to ignore you?

See Also ...

How to Get the Most Out of the Eucharist (Pages 67-72, "How Do We Respond?")

The Power of the Cross ("Day 22: The Cross of Christ Illumines Blindness")

20. HOW TO WITNESS THE BREAKING OF THE BREAD (Pages 197-202)

Meditation (Page 201)

Review Questions

1. What is the symbolism of the "breaking of the bread"?

2. What is the symbolism of the "co-mingling" rite?

3. What was called the *fermentum*, and what did it symbolize?

4. What does the priest pray that Body and Blood of Christ will bring to those who receive Him while placing a small piece of the Eucharist into the chalice containing the Precious Blood?

5. Where do the words of the "Lamb of God" prayer come from?

Reflection Questions

1. The disciples on the road to Emmaus on the day of the Resurrection walked with the Risen Christ but did not recognize Him until the "breaking of the bread." How did

this act help them to overcome their lack of insight into the Lord with whom they had journeyed seven miles?

2. How do the words of Saint John the Baptist, pointing out who Jesus was to those around him, fit with the action of the presider? What do they remind us of in regard to who Jesus is and who we are?

See Also …

How to Get the Most Out of the Eucharist (Pages 91-93, "Body and Blood for Life")

The Power of the Cross ("Thursday after Ash Wednesday: Jesus' Invitation")

21. HOW TO RECEIVE HOLY COMMUNION (Pages 203-211)

Meditation (Page 210)

Review Questions

1. Where do the words that the presider says as he holds up the Blessed Sacrament — "Behold the Lamb of God" and "Blessed are those who are called" — come from?
2. Where do the words that we say in response come from?
3. What is the "required disposition" to receive the Eucharist?
4. What do we give our assent to when we receive Holy Communion?
5. According to the *Catechism of the Catholic Church* what are the "fruits of Holy Communion"?
6. How did Saint Cyril of Jerusalem instruct the newly baptized Christians of the early Church to receive Communion?

Reflection Questions

1. What did Pope John Paul II mean when he wrote in *Ecclesia de Eucharistia* that at Communion we both receive and are received by Jesus?

2. How is "speaking the Bible" as we do with most of the prayers we say at Mass different from "praying with the Bible"?

3. How can contemplating the "fruits of Holy Communion," summarized from the *Catechism of the Catholic Church* in the chapter, help us to better appreciate and understand this great Sacrament that we receive?

4. How do you spend time in "thanksgiving" after receiving so great a Sacrament?

See Also ...

How to Get the Most Out of the Eucharist (Pages 103-112, "Commune: Receive the Eucharist")

The Power of the Cross ("Day 37: Taking Up Our Cross in Reverence")

22. HOW TO RECEIVE THE FINAL BLESSING (Pages 213-216)

Review Questions

1. In the example of a blessing in Scripture given in the Chapter, who is giving the blessing and what is the occasion?

2. What does the sending forth of the priest or deacon really mean?

Reflection Questions

1. How does the sending forth — "*Ite missa est*" — give us the sense that the Mass is all about being empowered for a mission given to us by Christ?

2. What does the chapter suggest should be our attitude toward those who leave Mass early? Have you ever left Mass early and why?

See Also ...

How to Get the Most Out of the Eucharist (Pages 116-120, "Matter of Life and Death" and "Go")

The Power of the Cross ("Day 1: The Cross of Christ Teaches Us Our Mission")

23. HOW TO LEAVE THE CHURCH AND EVANGELIZE (Pages 217-221)

Meditation (Page 220)

Review Questions

1. What is the mission that you have when you leave the church building?
2. What is a church bulletin and how can reading it help you to find opportunities to learn about your faith and learn about the needs of your parish?

Reflection Questions

1. What will you do with the Scripture readings you have heard at this Mass and the homily that has been preached?
2. What will you do with the Presence of the Lord that you carry within you?
3. Who do you know that needs to hear the "good news"?
4. Is there a person that would be helped by reading this book on the Mass? If so, consider passing it on to them.

See Also ...

How to Get the Most Out of the Eucharist (Pages 113-123, "Evangelize: Share the Good News")

The Power of the Cross ("Day 38: Taking Up Our Cross to Follow the Lord")

Appendix IV

——— Where Can I Learn More? ———

BOOKS

Akin, James. *Mass Confusion: The Do's and Don'ts of Catholic Worship*. San Diego, Calif.: Catholic Answers, 1998.

Aquilina, Mike. *The Mass of the Early Christians*. Huntington, Ind.: Our Sunday Visitor, 2000.

Arinze, Francis Cardinal. *The Holy Eucharist*. Huntington, Ind.: Our Sunday Visitor, 2001.

Arinze, Francis Cardinal. *Cardinal Reflections: Active Participation and the Liturgy*. Chicago: Hillenbrand Books, 2005.

Arinze, Francis Cardinal. *Celebrating the Holy Eucharist*. San Francisco: Ignatius Press, 2006.

Baker, Robert, and Benedict J. Groeschel. *When Did We See You, Lord?* Huntington, Ind.: Our Sunday Visitor, 2005.

Benedictine Monk, A. *Discovering the Mass*. London: St. Austin Press, 1949.

Benedictine Monk, A. *The Sacred Liturgy*. London: St. Austin Press, 1949.

Bouyer, Louis. *Eucharist: Theology and Spirituality of the Eucharistic Prayer*. Notre Dame, Ind.: University of Notre Dame Press, 1968.

Brown, Raymond. *New Testament Essays*. New York: Paulist Press, 1965.

Cabié, Robert. *The Church at Prayer: An Introduction to the Liturgy, Volume II, The Eucharist*. Translated by Matthew J. O'Connell; edited by Aimé Georges Martimort. Collegeville, Minn.: The Liturgical Press, 1986.

Casel, Odo. *The Mystery of Christian Worship*. New York: Herder and Herder, 1962.

Clark, Stephen B. *Catholics and the Eucharist: A Scriptural Introduction*. Ann Arbor, Mich.: Charis, 2000.

Crouan, Denis. *The History and the Future of the Roman Liturgy*. San Francisco: Ignatius Press, 2005.

Deiss, Lucien. *The Mass*. Collegeville, Minn.: The Liturgical Press, 1992.

Dodds, Bill, and Dale Fushek. *Your One-Stop Guide to the Mass*. Ann Arbor, Mich.: Charis, 2000.

Dubruiel, Michael. *The Church's Most Powerful Novenas*. Huntington, Ind.: Our Sunday Visitor, 2006.

Dubruiel, Michael. *How to Get the Most Out of the Eucharist*. Huntington, Ind.: Our Sunday Visitor, 2005.

Dubruiel, Michael. *The Pocket Guide to the Mass*. Huntington, Ind.: Our Sunday Visitor, 2007.

Dubruiel, Michael. *The Power of the Cross*. Huntington, Ind.: Our Sunday Visitor, 2004.

Dubruiel, Michael. *Praying in the Presence of Our Lord with Fulton J. Sheen*. Huntington, Ind., Our Sunday Visitor, 2002.

Dubruiel, Michael, and Welborn, Amy. *Praying the Rosary with the Joyful, Luminous, Sorrowful, and Glorious Mysteries*. Huntington, Ind.: Our Sunday Visitor, 2003.

Emminghaus, Johannes H. *The Eucharist: Essence, Form, Celebration*. Collegeville, Minn.: The Liturgical Press, 1978.

Fabing, Robert. *The Eucharist of Jesus: A Spirituality for Eucharistic Celebration*. Phoenix, Ariz.: Epoch Universal Publications, 1986.

Ferguson, George. *Signs & Symbols in Christian Art*. London: Oxford University Press, 1961.

Gortler, Rosemarie, and Donna Piscitelli. *The Mass Book for Children*. Huntington, Ind.: Our Sunday Visitor, 2004.

Greenberg, Blu. *How to Run a Traditional Jewish Household*. New York: Simon and Schuster, 1983.

Groeschel, Benedict, and James Monti. *In the Presence of Our Lord*. Huntington, Ind.: Our Sunday Visitor, 1997.

Groeschel, Benedict. *Praying in the Presence of Our Lord*. Huntington, Ind.: Our Sunday Visitor, 1999.

Groeschel, Benedict J,. and Robert J. Baker. *When Did We See You Lord?* Huntington, Ind.: Our Sunday Visitor, 2005.

Guardini, Romano. *The Spirit of the Liturgy.* New York: Herder and Herder, 1997.

Howard, Thomas. *If Your Mind Wanders at Mass.* San Francisco: Ignatius Press, 2001.

Isca, Kay Lynn. *Catholic Etiquette for Children at Mass.* Huntington, Ind.: Our Sunday Visitor, 2001.

Isca, Kay Lynn. *Catholic Etiquette: What You Need to Know About Catholic Rites and Wrongs.* Huntington, Ind.: Our Sunday Visitor, 1997.

Jungmann, Joseph A. *The Mass of the Roman Rite: Its Origin and Development, Volume I.* Dublin: Four Courts Press Ltd., 1951.

Jungmann, Joseph A. *The Mass of the Roman Rite: Its Origin and Development, Volume II.* Dublin: Four Courts Press Ltd., 1955.

Jurgens, William A. *The Faith of the Early Fathers: Volume One.* Collegeville, Minn.: The Liturgical Press, 1970.

Jurgens, William A. *The Faith of the Early Fathers: Volume Two.* Collegeville, Minn.: The Liturgical Press, 1979.

Jurgens, William A. *The Faith of the Early Fathers: Volume Three.* Collegeville, Minn.: The Liturgical Press, 1979.

Kane, John A. *Transforming Your Life through the Eucharist.* Manchester, N.H.: Sophia Press, 1999.

Knox, Ronald. *The Mass in Slow Motion.* New York: Sheed & Ward, 1948.

Lang, Uwe Michael. *Turning Towards the Lord: Orientation in Liturgical Prayer.* San Francisco: Ignatius. 2005.

Lindsey, Jacquelyn. *The Catholic Family Prayer Book.* Huntington, Ind.: Our Sunday Visitor, 2001.

Lukefahr, Oscar. *We Worship: A Guide to the Catholic Mass.* Liguori, Mo.: Ligouri, 2004.

Madrid, Patrick. *Why Is That in Tradition?* Huntington, Ind.: Our Sunday Visitor, 2002.

McBride, Alfred, O.Praem. *Celebrating the Mass: A Guide for Understanding and Loving the Mass More Deeply.* Huntington, Ind.: Our Sunday Visitor, 1999.

McGuckian, Michael. *The Holy Sacrifice of the Mass: A Search For an Acceptable Notion of Sacrifice.* Chicago: Hillenbrand Books, 2005.

Merton, Thomas. *The Living Bread.* New York: Farrar, Straus & Cudahy, 1956.

Miller, Charles E. *Liturgy for the People of God, Volume II: The Celebration of the Eucharist.* New York: Alba House, 2001.

Miller, Charles E. *Liturgy for the People of God, Volume III: Sacraments & Other Matters Liturgical.* New York: Alba House, 2001.

Montessori, Maria. *The Mass Explained to Children.* Fort Collins, Colo.: Roman Catholic Books, 1932.

Monti, James. *The Week of Salvation: History and Tradition of Holy Week.* Huntington, Ind.: Our Sunday Visitor, 1993.

Nichols, Aidan. *The Holy Eucharist: From the New Testament to Pope John Paul II.* Dublin: Veritas, 1991.

O'Connor, James T. *The Hidden Manna: A Theology of the Eucharist.* San Francisco: Ignatius, 1988.

Oury, Guy. *The Mass: Spirituality, History, Practice.* Translated by John Otto. New York: Catholic Book Publishing Co., 1988.

Paul, Archbishop of Finland. *The Feast of Faith: An Invitation to the Love Feast of the Kingdom of God.* Translated by Esther Williams. Crestwood, N.Y.: St. Vladimir's Seminary Press, 1988.

Pennington, M. Basil. *The Eucharist: Wine of Faith, Bread of Life.* Ligouri, Mo.: Ligouri/Triumph, 2000.

Randolph, Francis. *Know Him in the Breaking of the Bread: A Guide to the Mass.* San Francisco: Ignatius Press, 1994.

Ratzinger, Joseph Cardinal (Pope Benedict XVI). *Feast of Faith: Approaches to a Theology of the Liturgy.* Translated by Graham Harrison. San Francisco: Ignatius, 1986.

Ratzinger, Joseph Cardinal (Pope Benedict XVI). *God is Near: The Eucharist, the Heart of Life.* Translated by Henry Taylor. San Francisco: Ignatius, 2003.

Ratzinger, Joseph Cardinal (Pope Benedict XVI). *A New Song for the Lord: Faith in Christ and the Liturgy Today.* New York: Crossroad, 1996.

Ratzinger, Joseph Cardinal (Pope Benedict XVI). *The Spirit of the Liturgy.* Translated by John Saward. San Francisco: Ignatius, 2000.

Reid, Alcuin, O.S.B. *Looking Again at the Question of the Liturgy With Cardinal Ratzinger: Proceedings of the July 2001 Fontgombault Liturgical Conference.* Farmborough, Hampshire, England: Saint Michael's Abbey, 2004.

Reid, Alcuin, O.S.B. *The Organic Development of the Liturgy.* Farmborough, Hampshire, England: Saint Michael's Abbey, 2004.

Robinson, Jonathan. *The Mass and Modernity: Walking to Heaven Backward.* San Francisco: Ignatius, 2005.

Schmemann, Alexander. *The Eucharist: Sacrament of the Kingdom.* Crestwood, N.Y.: St. Vladimir's Seminary, 1988.

Schmemann, Alexander. *For the Life of the World: Sacraments and Orthodoxy.* Crestwood, N.Y.: St. Vladimir's Seminary, 1997.

Socias, James. *Daily Roman Missal.* Huntington, Ind.: Our Sunday Visitor, 1998.

Stravinskas, Peter M.J. *The Bible and the Mass.* Mount Pocono, Pa.: Newman House Press, 2000.

Stravinskas, Peter M.J. *The Catholic Church and the Bible.* San Francisco: Ignatius Press, 1987.

Stravinskas, Peter M.J. *Catholic Dictionary.* Huntington, Ind.: Our Sunday Visitor, 2002.

Thurian, Max. *The Mystery of the Eucharist.* Grand Rapids, Mich.: Eerdmans Publishing Co., 1984.

Von Speyr, Adrienne. *The Holy Mass.* Translated by Helena M. Saward. San Francisco: Ignatius Press, 1999.

Weber, Gerard P. *The Eucharist: A View from the Pew.* Cincinnati: St. Anthony Messenger Press, 2000.

Welborn, Amy. *Prove It! Prayer.* Huntington, Ind.: Our Sunday Visitor, 2002.

Welborn, Amy. *The Words We Pray: Discovering the Richness of Traditional Catholic Prayers.* Chicago: Loyola, 2005.

VIDEO/CD-ROM

A Walk Through the Mass with Bishop Donald W. Wuerl, Our Sunday
Visitor, Huntington, Ind., 1999.

*The Early Church Fathers on CD-ROM: Bringing You Closer to Your
Faith,* Harmony Media, Gervais, Ore., 2000.

Why We Go to Mass: Liturgy and Our Lives, J-Glenn Murray, Loyola
Press, Chicago, 2002.

INTERNET

Catechism of the Catholic Church (at the Vatican site)
www.vatican.va/archive/ENG0015/_INDEX.HTM

Christian Classics Ethereal Library (great resource for works of the
early Church fathers) **www.ccel.org/**

Compendium of the Catechism of the Catholic Church (at the Vatican
site)
**www.vatican.va/archive/compendium_ccc/documents/
archive_2005_compendium-ccc_en.html**

Ecclesia de Eucharistia, encyclical of Pope John Paul II on the
Eucharist, 2003 (at the Vatican site)
www.vatican.va/edocs/ENG0821/_INDEX.HTM

General Instruction of the Roman Missal, 2003 (at the United States
Conference of Catholic Bishops site)
www.nccbuscc.org/liturgy/current/revmissalisromanien.shtml

New Advent Catholic Encyclopedia (Their entry on the Mass provides an extensive history of the Mass.)
www.newadvent.org/cathen/09790b.htm

The New American Bible (at the United States Conference of
Catholic Bishops site) **www.nccbuscc.org/nab/**

Redemptionis Sacramentum, "On certain matters to be observed or to
be avoided regarding the Most Holy Eucharist," 2004 (at the
Vatican site)
**www.vatican.va/roman_curia/congregations/ccdds/
documents/rc_con_ccdds_doc_20040423_
redemptionis-sacramentum_en.html**

About the Author

Michael Dubruiel was the author of many books, including a sequel to this book, *How to Get the Most Out of the Eucharist*; a Lenten devotional, *The Church's Most Powerful Novenas*; and a Rosary prayer book co-authored with his wife, Amy Welborn, *Praying the Rosary With the Joyful, Luminous, Sorrowful, & Glorious Mysteries*.

He held a master's degree in Christian Spirituality from Creighton University in Omaha. At the time of his death in 2009, he was Director of Evangelization for the Diocese of Birmingham, Alabama. For more information on Michael and his books, see his website, http://www.michaeldubruiel.com or that of his wife Amy Welborn at http://www.amywelborn.com.